General Science:
Introductory Facts and Concepts
Volume Two

by

Katherine Davey

Julie Pigott

Irwin Worshell

ISBN 978-2-923623-74-0

Printed in Canada

Catalog Number: TBCE6-2

Reviewers:
Steve Brayne
Denis Lapierre

Editor-in-Chief:
Ernest Smith, Ph.D.

Copy Editors:
Ted Cooney
Joanne Labre

Design and Cover:
Saskia Nieuwendijk

Table of Contents

Table of Contents

ELECTRICITY

UNIT 1

Electricity

Lesson #1 – History of the Atom

Objectives:

- The development of the model of the atom.

- The difference between Aristotle & Democritus' view.

- Dalton's view of the atom.

- Thomson's modification to the model.

- Rutherford's experiment.

- Bohr's adjustment to the atom's model.

Introduction

You're reading this in a room lit by a light bulb while watching TV or listening to a stereo. The phone is ringing while the microwave is beeping that your soup is ready. You are surrounded by it. It is in almost every thing that touches your life. You probably could not function without it. But you can't see it.

The furnace or air conditioner that's keeping you warm or cold, can not really function without it. As you look around, you can hear the whirring of the refrigerator reminding you of the cool lemonade that's waiting for you. Yet the clock on the wall says that it's about time you started reading this unit. So you go over to the pencil sharpener you got for Christmas and sharpen a few pencils for the task. It's all around you and you still don't see it.

You're startled when a clap of thunder disturbs your thoughts. The lightning seemed to have come near the house. If you're lucky, the lights will stay on long enough for you to do at least the first section. Well, now you're getting the idea.

You can see it, sometimes that is. The lightning, the lights in the house, as well as all the other items mentioned above depend on the same phenomenon.

All these things have a very fundamental scientific, common principle. They all use electricity, or some form of electricity. How could you function without it? The answer is you can't! But what is electricity? You can't see it but it's there. How is it made? Where does it come from? How does it get to you? How do you control it? How could the thing that comes from such a small battery be the same thing that comes from the local power plant?

This unit will begin to uncover some of the principles behind electricity. Read on, using your lamp while listening to the latest on the radio.

The Origin of Electricity

To be able to understand electricity, you have to know where it comes from, what it's made of, how it moves and how to use it.

The first place to start is its origin. The origin of electricity is like everything else in the world. It is based on matter. Theoretically all matter in the universe was created at the "big bang" and we have been rearranging matter ever since.

The Atom

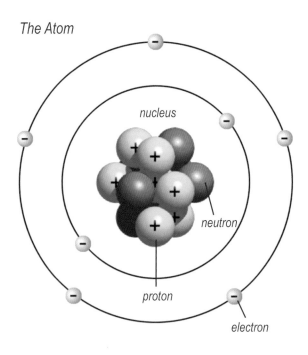

To find the true source of electricity, we must look into the structure of matter. We must look at its fundamental building blocks. Matter has always been a puzzle to man. Many have tried various ways to explore what it is made of with only limited success. Only a small piece of the puzzle has been revealed at any one time.

Greek philosophers were the first to study matter. Their concepts, however, were based on theorizing and not on experimentation. We know that great debates raged between the different schools of thought concerning the very nature of the world. The leaders of two of the most prominent schools of thought were Democritus and Aristotle.

It was thought that the world was composed of what you could actually sense around you: the AIR that could be felt as wind, the EARTH beneath your feet, the WATER around you, and, finally, FIRE. It was argued that all objects were composed of some amount of each of these four elements.

It could be argued that all objects were composed of some amount of each of these four elements. Depending on the varying

proportions, all types of substances could be explained. Rock would have more earth and wine would certainly have water and maybe even some fire. Without the proper tools at their disposal, it would be difficult to challenge the assertion that all matter is composed of the four elements – earth, air, fire and water.

Aristotle
(384-322 BC)

Greek philosopher and scientist. Once referred to as, "The man of all knowledge", Aristotle provided answers for global phenomenon that were popular for over 2000 years. He reasoned that "heavier" objects fell to the ground faster than "lighter" objects. Aristotle also conceived the universe consisting of celestial spheres. Aristotle was also a supporter of a geocentric model of the universe: meaning he thought the Earth was at the center of the universe. His theories of motion included all motion on the Earth to be straight and linear, whereas motion in the heavens (above the Earth) was circular. Of course with the revelations by Galileo and Newton, all of Aristotle's laws have become obsolete. He is still however respected for his many contributions to the field of philosophy.

Aristotle was not primarily a mathematician but made important contributions by systematizing deductive logic. He wrote on physical subjects: some parts of his Analytica posteriora show an unusual grasp of the mathematical method. Primarily, however, he is important in the development of all knowledge.

Democritus
(460-370 BCE)

Democritus was one of the first Greek philosophers to propose an atomic model. Democritus believed all matter was discontinuous. He called the smallest unit of matter atom, from the Greek atomos, meaning "indivisible". These atoms were small objects that made up all matter, and could not be divided into smaller form. According to Democritus, atoms were identical, however, their arrangement could explain the difference between the characteristics of one substance and those of another.

To add to the idea of the day, it was felt that since all things were composed of the same starting materials, there were no gaps. All matter was continuous. No empty space could exist, since all substances were connected somehow to each other. The concept of a space, a vacuum, was actually quite unsettling and difficult to imagine. Any theory that proposed this notion really didn't stand much of a chance. Yet, there were those that dreamt beyond what could be seen and felt.

Democritus was such a philosopher. He proposed that since sand existed in smaller and smaller particles, it could be said that all matter could be broken down into smaller and smaller units. The smallest unit that could not be divided any further would be called the atom (*atomos* in Greek). Unfortunately, there was no way to "see" these atoms. This theory would also mean that there would be spaces between the atoms and thus this "discontinuous" model did not win over many converts.

At this time it was also observed that a substance called amber (the fossilized sap of trees) had very peculiar properties. When rubbed with fur, the amber would attract small bits of material or paper. These observations would eventually lead to a deeper understanding of the structure of the atom. The structure of matter was merely a debate. No actual testing of the theories took place, because philosophy, not science, ruled the day.

So, let's skip ahead to an era where scientists were probing into the nature of matter once again. This time they were using experimental observations. Discoveries that included some of the basic elements – oxygen, nitrogen, hydrogen, etc. had led to the dropping of the notion of earth, wind, fire and water being elements. Instead, it was becoming increasingly obvious that matter was more complex. Yet, there were scientists, such as John Dalton, who felt that all the behaviors that substances exhibited could be explained by a fundamental structure of matter.

Dalton's theory stated that the smallest particle of a substance was indestructible, a theory similar to Democritus' atom. Each atom of a particular element would have to be identical so that when experiments were repeated, the results would never vary. Different elements would have to have different atoms. Their size and arrangement would help to explain why sulfur was yellow and oxygen was a gas. When these elements reacted together, it was possible to create two or more different products. These products were always found to have a

Dalton, *John*
(1766-1844)

British chemist and physicist who developed the atomic theory of matter and hence is known as one of the fathers of modern physical science.

whole number ratio when combining the reactants. This evidence supported Dalton's notion of the atom as an indestructible solid particle.

In the years following, Franklin and others conducted experiments with electricity and found some rather shocking things. These facts supported the Greek's *elektron* (amber) effect and showed that matter could be electrically charged. Franklin believed that this

Franklin, *Benjamin*
(1706-1790)

Famous for being a scientist, an inventor, a statesman, a printer, a philosopher, a musician, and an economist.

electricity was a fluid that was passed from substance to substance. A deficit of this "fluid" would be considered negative (a loss) and an excess of the fluid would be considered positive (a gain). He was definitely on the right track. Even though he got it backwards, the concept of loss and gain is fundamental to electricity.

So where did this loss and gain come from? Other scientists were working on electrical discharge tubes, a sort of lightning in a bottle. J.J. Thomson explored a form of ray tube that showed rays always emanating from the negative end (the cathode, hence the name **cathode ray tube**). His experiments were able to determine that the rays always had the same properties regardless of the material used as the cathode. These rays always had the same properties. The conclusion? All substances contained these negative particles which were named electrons. They appeared to be extremely small and had almost no mass. Based on experiments with lightning and other observations, electrons were found to be plentiful in matter. The electron was a fundamental building block of matter.

Thomson believed that the atom was divisible. The atom contained a small negative particle that could be removed from the atom leaving behind a hard positive core. Thomson also believed that the atom must also contain something that neutralizes this negatively charged subatomic particle. He suggested his "plum pudding" model where the electrons were scattered among positive

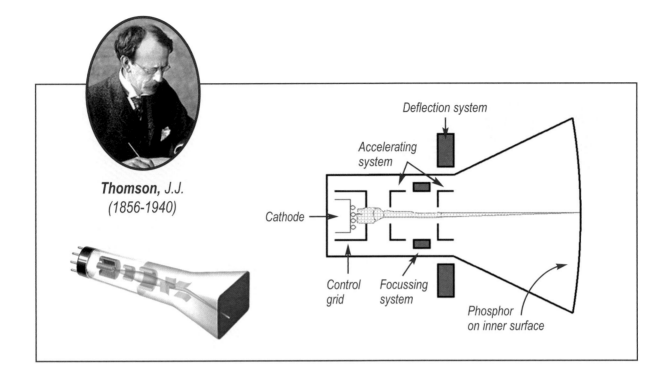

Thomson, J.J.
(1856-1940)

Deflection system

Accelerating system

Cathode

Control grid

Focussing system

Phosphor on inner surface

charges. The atom was divisible; it contained a small negative charge that could be removed from the atom leaving behind a positive charge. Dalton's model had to be modified.

So, was this the definitive description of the atom? Radioactivity would be used to get closer to an answer. Radioactivity was being investigated but was misunderstood. Minerals that glowed were believed to be radiating sunlight that they had absorbed. During some

bad weather a discovery was made that these glowing minerals were actually present in the rocks. It seemed that matter itself was breaking down. Through much investigation, the nature of this radiation started to shed light on the basic structure of matter.

Ernest Rutherford used radiation to "look" inside the atom. In the same way that if you shot pellets at a chain link fence and would expect not to get hit by a ricochet, that's what happened when radiation was aimed at a thin sheet of gold foil. The vast majority of these particles passed right through and were unaffected. An occasional deflection of a charged particle back toward the start indicated that the metal foil was really a lot of empty space but had some very, very small yet hard and heavy particles inside. Rutherford proposed that the model of the atom contained a small,

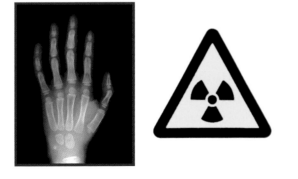

heavy nucleus at the center of the atom which was surrounded by a cloud of loosely held electrons (those negative particles from the cathode ray tube). This was in fact a major step towards the understanding of the atom's structure but still, there were some unanswered questions.

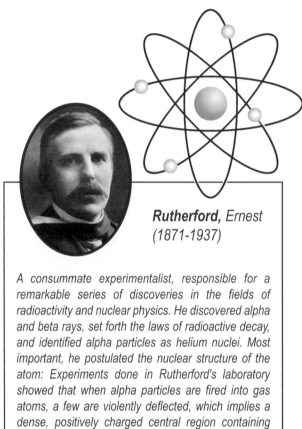

Rutherford, *Ernest*
(1871-1937)

A consummate experimentalist, responsible for a remarkable series of discoveries in the fields of radioactivity and nuclear physics. He discovered alpha and beta rays, set forth the laws of radioactive decay, and identified alpha particles as helium nuclei. Most important, he postulated the nuclear structure of the atom: Experiments done in Rutherford's laboratory showed that when alpha particles are fired into gas atoms, a few are violently deflected, which implies a dense, positively charged central region containing most of the atomic mass.

Niels Bohr applied some phenomenal mathematics to explain why the electrons didn't crash into the nucleus and why when atoms are excited (given extra energy), different atoms emit different colors. His theory was similar to the solar system which has each planet moving in a predetermined orbit around the sun based on a mathematical equation. The current belief is that around the positive nucleus are negative electrons moving around in special orbitals. All atoms will have at least one electron in an outside orbit.

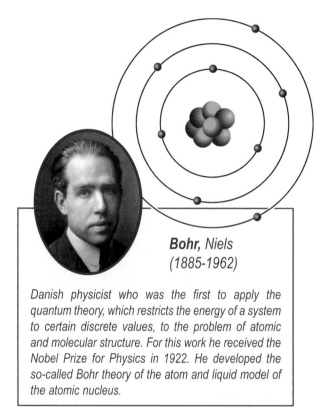

Bohr, *Niels*
(1885-1962)

Danish physicist who was the first to apply the quantum theory, which restricts the energy of a system to certain discrete values, to the problem of atomic and molecular structure. For this work he received the Nobel Prize for Physics in 1922. He developed the so-called Bohr theory of the atom and liquid model of the atomic nucleus.

That is the point of this section. These outside (valence) electrons are in essence, "up for grabs". They can be exchanged and moved around to create the electricity we use every day. Simply put, moving electrons from atom to atom is electricity. Now, we have a basis for understanding some of the experiments involving electricity.

Lesson # 2 – Electrostatics

Objectives:

- The two categories of substances.

- The nature of static charge.

- The types of electrostatics.

- How grounding occurs.

Movement of Electrons

Now that you understand a little about the atom, we are ready to look at the movement of the outer (valence) electrons. First, we have to look at the two categories of materials we are going to deal with. Those that allow for the movement of these electrons and those that do not.

The materials that allow the movement of electrons are called **conductors**. These are substances that have atoms whose outer electron(s) can move relatively easily between atoms. The material tends to be made of metallic atoms though not exclusively. You're certainly aware of metals such as copper and aluminum used in electrical wiring. It is also true that you can get electricity to move through materials such as graphite (the main ingredient in the "lead" in your pencil). The structure of these substances at the atomic level, lend themselves to having electrons move between atoms.

The other category of substances is called **insulators**. These materials tend to be solids that do not have electrons that are free to move around from atom to atom. Instead, the nature of the atoms tends to be non-metallic. They hold onto

graphite / conductor

wire / conductor

sole / insulator

glass / insulator

their electrons for dear life. Rubber is an example and the soles on your shoes can help you avoid some pretty nasty shocks. Glass and plastic electrons don't move easily so these materials are used in electrical devices to make sure the electricity goes where it should.

The valence electrons (outermost orbiting electrons) are waiting but will not jump from one atom to another on their own. Something must be done to get things started. When materials are rubbed together a transfer of electrons will occur. The insulator will "steal" electrons from the conductor. That makes sense since one holds onto its electrons and the other allows them "movement". The picture gets more complicated when two insulators are rubbed together.

What happens when glass is rubbed with silk? The rubbing brings the materials close enough together for the atoms to interact with each other. Some electrons will move during this encounter. But which way? Which substance gets the electron, which loses? When lots of substances are tested in pairs, it is found that some keep their electrons better than others do while some materials tend to lose their electrons. It's like a tug of war. The substances that can hold onto electrons will acquire them from the "losers". In this way, they

will become **negatively** charged. With extra electrons on their surface, these objects will have a negative aura. This is called a **static charge** (since it's not moving).

Meanwhile, the material that lost its electrons has a surface with not enough electrons. This lack of electrons creates a positive charge to occur. The **positive** glow comes from deep inside the atoms' nuclei. Thus, every time electrons are transferred in this way, two charged objects are "created". The truth is that charges have been separated and as in life, things like to get back to the way they were. Nature exists in a balance of negative and positive charges. The charged objects that we've just created may not stay that way for long.

Since the electrons were taken forcibly from one substance to another, there will be an attraction to send them back from where they came. You've heard of opposites attracting? This is it. The

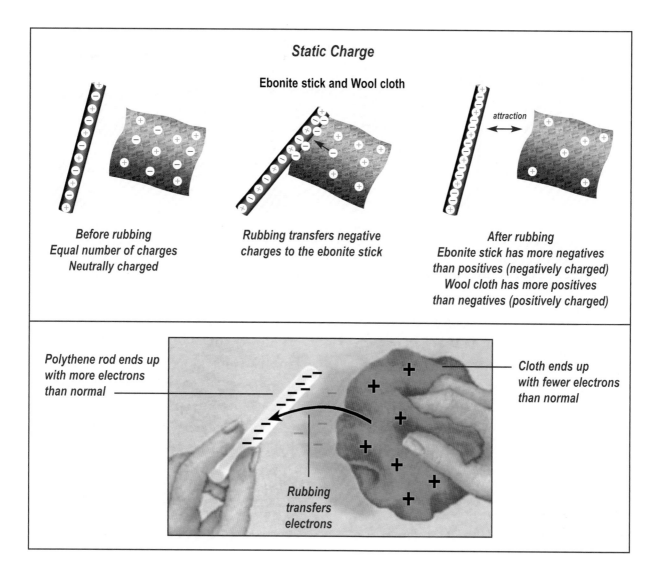

Static Charge

Ebonite stick and Wool cloth

Before rubbing
Equal number of charges
Neutrally charged

Rubbing transfers negative charges to the ebonite stick

attraction

After rubbing
Ebonite stick has more negatives than positives (negatively charged)
Wool cloth has more positives than negatives (positively charged)

Polythene rod ends up with more electrons than normal

Cloth ends up with fewer electrons than normal

Rubbing transfers electrons

positively charged object will attract the negatively charged object, in an attempt to regain its lost electrons. This behavior is the first law in electrostatics; (materials that have opposite charges will attract each other.) In addition, those that have the same charge, will repel each other. That is the second law of electrostatics. As a matter of fact, the positively charged object will try to get electrons from just about anywhere. Putting a charged cloth down on a table will give it a chance to steal away a couple of electrons. Lint, small pieces of paper, things like that are all fair game.

Eventually, all substances will return to the normal neutral state. In nature there will always be the same number of positive charges as there are negative charges. How the charges are distributed determines if objects are neutral or charged.

While objects are charged, it may be difficult to tell that they are in fact electrically charged. To detect whether the object is charged or not, we can use a device called an electroscope. It is a device that responds to the presence of a charged object.

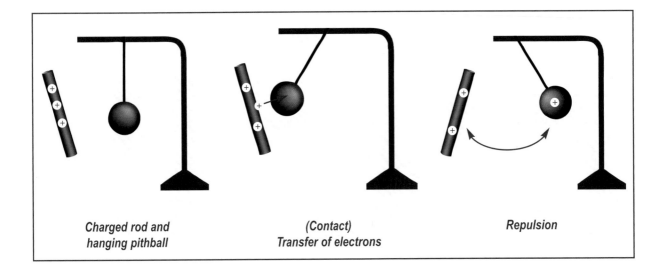

Charged rod and hanging pithball

(Contact) Transfer of electrons

Repulsion

The pithball electroscope is really simple. A light, small ball made of pith (the heartwood of a tree) is coated with metal paint or foil and is suspended on an insulated thread. When a charged object is held nearby, the ball will tend to swing over to the charge. As long as it doesn't make contact, it will be attracted to either charge (positive or negative). If contact is made, then it will become the same charge as what touched it. During contact, or even in very close proximity, electrons will jump from one object to the other to try to even out the charge. Once it has acquired the same charge it will now be repelled.

It is interesting to watch the pithball first being attracted and then repelled. By thinking back to the structure of the atom, this reaction can be explained. If a positively charged object (one that is missing one or more electrons) is brought near a neutral pithball, it tries to pull off some of the pithball's electrons. Generally, there won't be enough strength to pull this off. As the pithball gets close enough and finally touches, then some of the electrons are actually taken away from the pithball. Usually, not enough electrons are transferred, leaving both objects now charged. Repulsion occurs. Negatively charged objects follow the same pattern but the electrons go the other way, that is, from the negatively charged object to the pithball.

A second type of electroscope is a little more elaborate. It is called a metal leaf electroscope. It consists of a metal knob at the end of a metal rod, which is placed through an insulting cork or stopper. The rod extends down into a chamber (like a bottle). At the bottom end of the rod, there is a thin foil of gold or aluminum. This foil is like an upside down V. When a charged object is brought near the top knob, a movement of electrons occurs along the whole rod and foil. The two leaves of the V will both become the same charge and will repel each other. In this way, you can check if an object is charged or not. The more they repel, the greater the charge on the object.

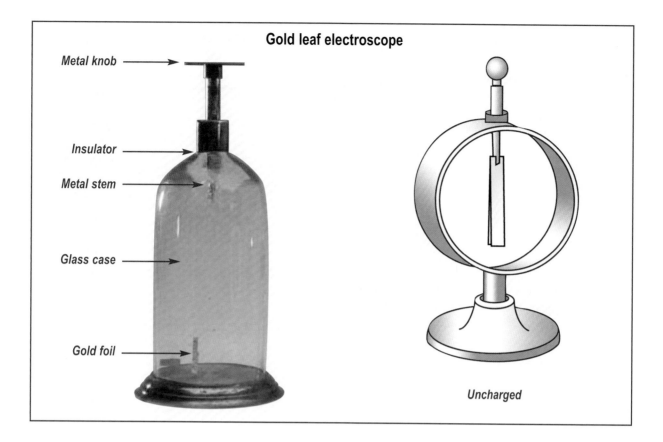

Gold leaf electroscope

Metal knob

Insulator

Metal stem

Glass case

Gold foil

Uncharged

This leaf separation occurs by a process called induction. The nearness of the charged object will either draw electrons up to the knob or repel them down towards the ends of the leaves. Either way, the leaves temporarily acquire a charge and repel each other. When the charged object is removed, there is no longer a force moving the electrons and they return to their usual position on their own atom. If on the other hand, contact is made, then electrons are either taken away or jump over to the electroscope. The electroscope will now be missing electrons or have too many. In either case, the electrons that are there on the surface are spread as evenly as possible over the entire metal rod. The leaves will both be either negative or positive, it depends on whether electrons were added to the electroscope

or removed from it. Either way you will see them spread apart indicating presence of charge. This leaf separation is brought about by conduction. The touching of the charged material to the knob allows electrons to be conducted from one to the other. The charge left behind on the electroscope is the same as that of the original charged object.

A bit of "magic" can be produced on this type of electroscope. We use both induction and conduction to charge the electroscope. The process involves "following the moving electrons". Say we start with a positively charged object. As we bring it near the knob of the electroscope, electrons are attracted up to the knob and away from the leaves causing them to become positive. The leaves repel each other and form the "V",

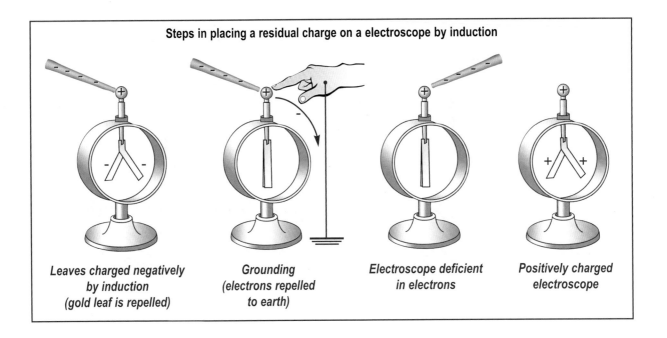

Steps in placing a residual charge on a electroscope by induction

Leaves charged negatively by induction (gold leaf is repelled)

Grounding (electrons repelled to earth)

Electroscope deficient in electrons

Positively charged electroscope

indicating charge. They try to pull the electrons back from the knob but can't win the tug of war. So where are the electrons going to come from? The answer: your finger.

Your finger could lose a few electrons without this loss being noticed. When your finger touches the side of the knob, extra electrons are moved from you into the electroscope and down to the positive leaves, making them neutral. This is a process called grounding. Any relatively large object can always spare or accept a few electrons. Due to this transfer, the leaves collapse and the electroscope looks neutral again. But extra electrons have been transferred to the scope?

As soon as you move the original charged object away from the knob, the leaves "magically" spread apart again. The reason is that the positively charged object held electrons in place on the knob while the extra electrons moved down to

ground the leaves. Once the charged object is removed these electrons are now "free" to spread out along the surface of the rod. The entire electroscope has an excess of electrons with the leaves indicating this by their V shape. The electroscope has been charged oppositely to that of the starting charged object. The process is called charging by induction since that's what kept the charges in place to start with. If you start with a negatively charged object, the electrons would move into your finger and therefore a positively charged electroscope is left behind.

As just mentioned, a process of grounding was used to get rid of a charged situation. Grounding can occur quickly as in the case of the electroscope or very slowly as in the discharging of a balloon that was rubbed against someone's hair and then placed on the wall. The name for discharging, getting back to neutral, sounds pretty obvious.

Grounding isn't the only way to neutralize a charged object. As mentioned, you could be the source of the "ground". Have you ever been zapped by a doorknob or the TV screen? The "zapping" is the jumping of electrons either away from or onto your finger. These are examples of grounding. For example, the screen has the charge and you provide the ground. With the doorknob, you are the charged object with the knob providing ground.

The type of object being grounded and its shape affect how easily grounding can take place. A TV screen only discharges at the point of contact. A metal doorknob discharges both sides at the same time. Metallic items will conduct the charge all along their length whereas insulators will only discharge at the area grounded.

Grounding also occurs slowly when the air around the charge is used to either receive or donate some electrons. All air contains particles and molecules that can help in the process of discharging. The shape of the charged object that comes into contact with the air also has an effect on the rate of grounding. The more pointed the surface of the object, the more concentrated the charge will be. With the charge more concentrated, there will be more attraction/repulsion with the surrounding air thus speeding up the process.

When an enormous number of electrons try to go to ground, it may create a spark. This occurs when enough electrons jump the gap through the air. As they move,

they ionize (make it charged) the air and produce a great deal of heat. The surrounding air expands quickly setting up a sound wave- the snap. As well, some of the air molecules may produce a flash of light (spark). If charge continues to build up and be discharged in an area, arcing may occur. The surrounding air will have more charged particles and thus speed up the time between discharges. Heat can also build up and may lead to a fire.

The greatest display of a grounding discharge is of course lightning. In the formation of a rain cloud, air currents move up and down within the cloud. This causes friction between the currents and sets up a separation of charge. The bottom of the cloud will induce charges on the earth and buildings below. The more pointed the object and the taller it is, the more likely it will be the location of discharge, the bolt of lightning. To protect houses and buildings, lightning rods protrude above the top of the roof

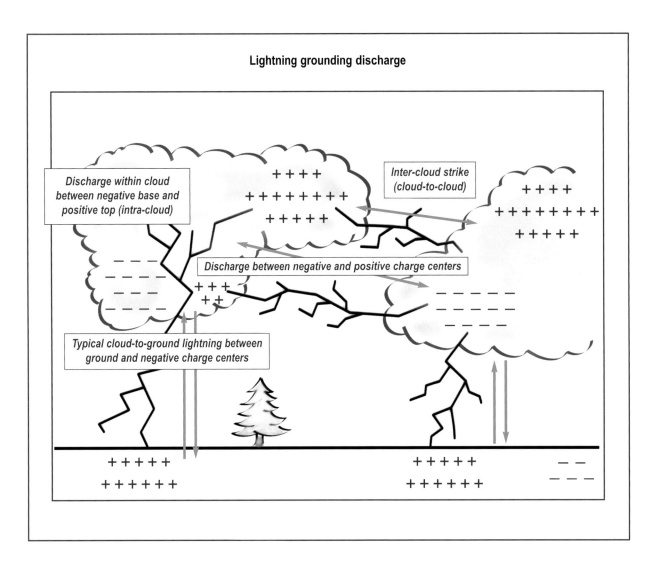

Lightning grounding discharge

Discharge within cloud between negative base and positive top (intra-cloud)

Inter-cloud strike (cloud-to-cloud)

$+ + + +$
$+ + + + + + +$
$+ + + + +$

$+ + + +$
$+ + + + + + +$
$+ + + + +$

$- - - -$
$- - - -$
$- - - -$

Discharge between negative and positive charge centers

$+ + +$
$+ +$

$- - - -$
$- - - -$
$- - - -$

Typical cloud-to-ground lightning between ground and negative charge centers

$+ + + + +$
$+ + + + +$

$+ + + + +$
$+ + + + +$

$- -$
$- - -$

and the base is buried in the ground. The hope is that the discharge will occur onto the rod instead of the roof. Of course there is no guarantee that nature will comply but at least it is safer.

This section can't be completed without a mention of the controlled lightning that you may have experienced. The "hair-raising" machine, the Van de Graaf generator, is the device that can create lightning. It uses the process of moving an insulated belt past a metal charging comb. As the belt moves upward, it transfers the charge to a second comb,

which deposits it on the dome. You know the one? When you place your hands on top and turn on the machine, it turns into a real hair raising experience.

Even though this section has included examples of charges (namely electrons) moving from place to place, either in small groups or in large lightning bolts, the basic premise is the separation of charge. Creating two oppositely charged areas sets up the "potential" for the charges to move. The next section will examine the phenomenon of moving charges in more detail.

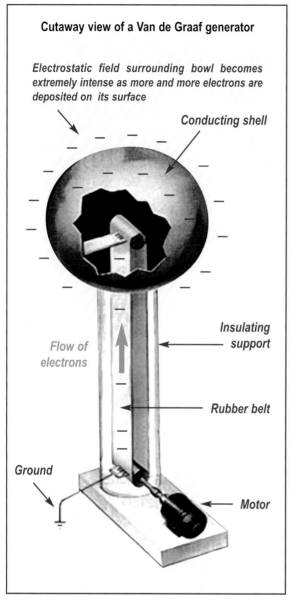

Cutaway view of a Van de Graaf generator

Electrostatic field surrounding bowl becomes extremely intense as more and more electrons are deposited on its surface

Conducting shell

Insulating support

Flow of electrons

Rubber belt

Ground

Motor

Van de Graaf with original generator

Lesson # 3 - Moving Charges

Objectives:

- Voltage and current.

- The different types of batteries.

- Other methods to get electrons moving.

In the previous section, we explored static charge. Although there was some movement of the electrons, as when a doorknob zaps you, the basic nature of the charges is that they are stuck wherever they are positioned on insulators. It is now time to get things moving. It is time to see how we can propel these electrons that really don't want to be together according to the law of electrostatics.

When charges are accumulated in a location, as in collecting electrons on a rubbed balloon, the effect may be that you can stick this balloon on the wall. The truth is that the electrons do not want to be stuck on the surface of the balloon. When given the opportunity, these electrons find other atoms and molecules to attach themselves to. If, on the other hand, these electrons were located on a conductor, there would be the possibility of movement along the conductor. Eventually, the movement might stop but if there was a way to recycle these electrons, get them to

follow the flow again, we might have something.

By accepting the notion that the combination of electrons and a conductor have the makings for a flow of charge, we see all that is missing is the reason for the charge to flow. So what would make electrons move from a location? Pressure. That's the answer. When too many electrons are collected at a point they apply a "pressure" on each other by electrical repulsion. The work and energy it may have taken to accumulate the electrons at this point can be returned by allowing the electrons to flow. The flow can occur, as it did with lightning, in an uncontrolled manner; or through a conductor, such as a wire leading to a light bulb, in a controlled manner.

To understand the flow of charge, which is called current, we need to look at some ways for accumulating the charge to flow; a way to measure how much flow there is and how much work (energy) is involved. First, we'll look at some ways of creating the pressure to move the electrons. Think of this like trying to get toothpaste to move. It doesn't want to move on its own but given the proper squeeze, it is possible to get some movement. When the pressure is released, the flow ceases. The same is true with electricity. Current stops flowing when the pressure, the battery, dies out.

A battery isn't the only way to get current moving. As we saw in the last section, friction can accumulate charge in one spot. Once "stored", this charge can be released or allowed to flow where it is needed. Rubbing fur and a rod will not create enough energy to separate a usable amount of charge. On the other hand, the Van de Graaf Generator, is a large-scale version of friction at work. The accumulation of separated charge can be very significant. From only a small number of electrons in balloons to millions upon millions in the Van de Graaf to 10^{20} (that's a 1 followed by 20 zeroes) electrons when lightning strikes. These situations tend to be unreliable and inconsistent.

To create a steady pressure, a more precise and dependable method was developed. AlessandroVolta produced the first steady flow of electric current by chemical means using a device called a voltaic pile, a forerunner of the electric battery. Using a salt solution and two strips of metals, copper and zinc, he was able to generate a potential difference between the electrons. With the salt

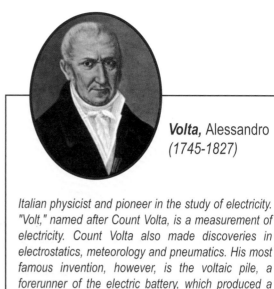

Volta, Alessandro
(1745-1827)

Italian physicist and pioneer in the study of electricity. "Volt," named after Count Volta, is a measurement of electricity. Count Volta also made discoveries in electrostatics, meteorology and pneumatics. His most famous invention, however, is the voltaic pile, a forerunner of the electric battery, which produced a steady stream of electricity.

solution acting as the "go between" the electrons are separated between the copper and the zinc. There is an accumulation of electrons on the zinc, making it the negative terminal whereas the copper, having lost its electrons, accumulates a positive charge. The individual reactions set up the separation of charges but does not create current. Similar to the toothpaste tube, you can squeeze all you want, but unless you open the top, it won't flow.

Today, Volta's experiment can be repeated using a device known as **voltaic cell.** One type of voltaic cell is the wet cell. A wet cell is composed of two strips of metals (electrodes) in an electrolyte, a liquid that conducts electricity. The electrolyte is usually an acidic medium. For electricity to flow it has to have someplace to go. Not until the two electrodes are connected will there be a current flowing (more of this later). This first **wet** cell showed the way

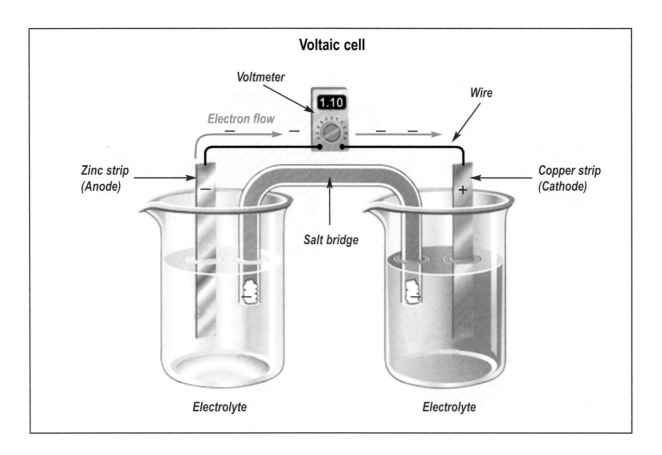

Voltaic cell

Voltmeter

1.10

Electron flow

Wire

Zinc strip
(Anode)

Copper strip
(Cathode)

−

+

Salt bridge

Electrolyte

Electrolyte

to set up a separation of charge between two terminals in a controlled manner. It was (is) called a wet cell due to the electrolytic solution needed to connect the two terminals. Its major drawback, as you probably can tell, is that it is wet. The electrolyte, which can be corrosive, can spill. The terminals, mainly the zinc plate, react with the electrolyte and eventually must be replaced.

A more familiar type of battery is also a more practical type. The **dry** cell is the next step up. One obvious advantage of the dry cell is, of course, that it's dry. It's not totally dry as there is a paste that is damp and it is the paste that contains the electrolyte inside the battery. Often, carbon is used as an electrode but recent changes have allowed for many different

formulations and combinations. A small watch battery tends to have silver oxide opposite a zinc electrode whereas an alkaline battery has manganese dioxide against a zinc powder. These types of batteries do eventually run out of electrochemical energy (the ability to push the electrons around) and have to be disposed of carefully, not recharged. Recharging these types of batteries could cause a build up of heat and internal gas. The result could be an explosion. Secondary cells on the other hand can be recharged.

The secondary cell works on the principle that the chemical reactions at the two terminals are reversible. By sending electricity to the battery, the reactions are reversed and new energy

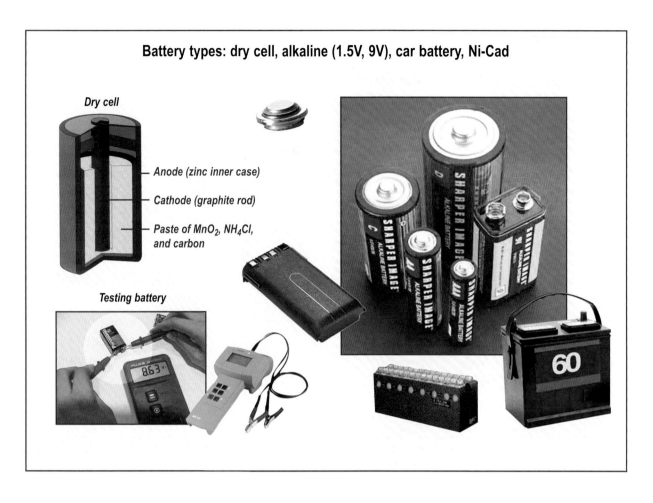

Battery types: dry cell, alkaline (1.5V, 9V), car battery, Ni-Cad

Dry cell

Anode (zinc inner case)

Cathode (graphite rod)

Paste of MnO_2, NH_4Cl, and carbon

Testing battery

is stored for use later. It's like winding the rubber band on the model plane you might have had when you were small. Until you release the propeller, the energy is stored inside. You were the source of the original energy, whereas in batteries the original energy starts with chemical reactions moving the electrons around. Ni-cad dry cells are a prime example of this type of battery. Even though it does contain liquid, your car battery falls into the same category of being rechargeable.

When batteries are combined, they can be placed together in two different ways. If they are connected end to end (positive to negative) as in most walkmans, etc, they pool their force and provide a greater push. The stacking of batteries is called series. In this way two 1.5 V batteries can produce a total voltage of 3 V. When the batteries are set up side by side with both positive ends connected to the holder and the same for the negative ends, each battery provides electrons to the circuit. The pressure is not greater, more electrons are available for the circuit and will in that case last longer. This type of side by side connection is called parallel.

Other methods are available for separating charge. Some are on a small scale whereas others produce enough charge separation for use by an entire city. The small variety includes the use of special crystals such as quartz and

Rochelle salt. When these crystals are squeezed or pressed, they release electrons. This effect is known as piezoelectricity. In the old days (and seen in recent resurgences of rap music), there is the use of a turntable fitted with a needle pickup that converts the minute vibrations into electrical signals that are sent to the amplifier for "modification". Using the same principle, when the trigger is pulled on a BBQ lighter, the crystal creates a spark, and a discharge of electricity is produced. Another less commercial method of producing a current flow is created

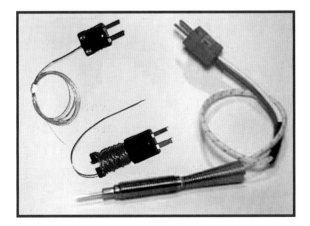

when two wires of different metals are joined to form a closed loop. When there is a difference in temperature between the two junctions, say one end is placed in a flame, a current is produced. This is useful in things like thermometers.

On a larger, and more important, scale is using the sun's energy to get the electrons to move. Solar power involves trapping the energy in the sun's rays and converting this into useful electrical energy. Solar panels are covered with cells that trap the sunlight. The energy in the radiation is absorbed by some of the outer electrons of the atoms, giving them enough energy to move freely. By pointing your calculator towards the light, you are "powering up" the photoelectric cell. When enough cells are connected together, it is possible to power more than just a calculator. Since the photo sensitive material can be made very thin and light, it is perfect to be used as a replacement for batteries aboard satellites and space stations.

The most important method for getting electrons to move is based on a discovery made a few hundred years ago. When a conductor is moved through a magnetic field, a current is produced. The magnetic field provides the push that moves the electrons through the wire. This is the principle of electromagnetic induction. Once you set up the wire around a spinning magnet or a coil between magnetic poles, the only thing missing is a method for spinning the magnet or coil. There used to be a device called a dynamo that would be positioned

St.Louis Motor

headlight. On a much larger scale, if you harness the falling water of Niagara, it would be able to turn huge coils. These types of gigantic generators provide power for entire regions.

The concept discussed in all of these methods for getting the electrons to move has been the same: produce a "pressure" that tries to force the electrons to follow a path through a circuit. Now that we haved looked at all these methods for getting the electrons ready for movement, it is time to discover where these electrons can travel and how we control the flow.

on the fork of a bicycle so that it could be pressed against the rotating tire. Once in motion, there would be electricity to run a

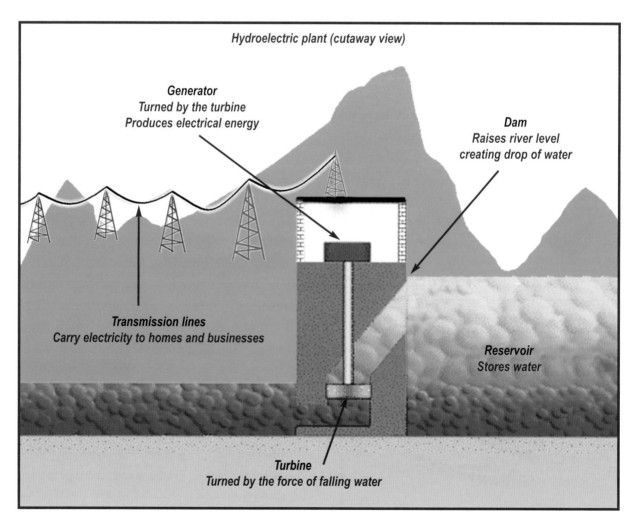

Hydroelectric plant (cutaway view)

Generator
Turned by the turbine
Produces electrical energy

Dam
Raises river level
creating drop of water

Transmission lines
Carry electricity to homes and businesses

Reservoir
Stores water

Turbine
Turned by the force of falling water

Lesson # 4 – The Circuit

As we have seen, there are many ways to get the electrons ready to flow. We always start with a power source, such as a dry cell battery. For the electrons to actually move, we need a conductor for the electrons to pass through. If we connect the two ends of the battery together, we will have completed our first circuit, although not a very useful one.

When contact is made, the pressure that the battery has set up on the electrons forces them into the wire. The advancing electrons from the battery push along the electrons that are already in the wire. This forces electrons out of the other end of the wire and into the positive end of the battery. This is like turning on the water tap at one end of the hose which will force water out the other end of the hose.

This is a short circuit indeed. The movement of the electrons is so fast that it produces friction within the wire. The wire in turn heats up rapidly. The likelihood is that the wire will melt and break. Once there is a break in the wire, the electrons can no longer continue to flow. The circuit is dead and you may also have a fire on your hands. This circuit does, or rather did, have all the components necessary for current to flow but the energy that the battery provided was wasted.

A much better setup would be to make good use of the electrons energy. A power source such as a battery is still needed as are insulating materials to contain the entire device. Say we use a small light bulb screwed into an insulated base, which has two conducting wires extending from either side. The other ends of these wires are then connected to the ends of a battery. When this is done, what you have is a simple flashlight. If you include a switch, you have a standard simple circuit.

The sample circuit must have the following components:

1- A source, which is the battery;

2- A load, to use up the energy being delivered by the current, which is the light bulb;

3- Conducting material to connect the various components together.

4- A switch and insulating materials are a bonus.

This circuit can be diagrammed using symbols. The circuit diagram allows for a clear representation of the connections and elements in the circuit. Sometimes in real life the wires can all be crossed, which would make it difficult to follow the flow. The diagram is also useful in that it allows us to check where to position the various meters we need to monitor the circuit.

Once the circuit is up and running, a current is flowing through the wires and energy is being used up. By using specialized meters, it is possible to measure the flow of the charge and, with a second meter, to measure the loss of energy as the current moves throughout the circuit. With these two measurements, other values could be determined, such as the power rating for a light bulb. More on this later.

To understand the significance of the values, you need to know what they represent and the units they are

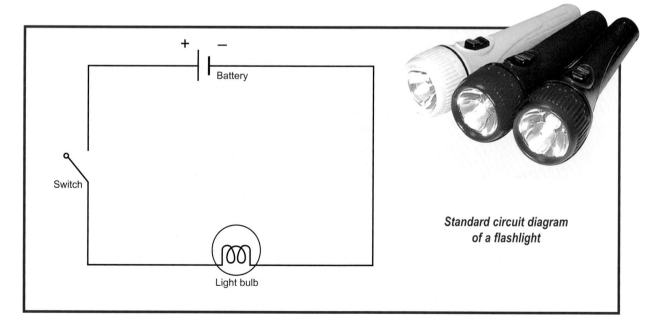

Standard circuit diagram of a flashlight

measured in. Let's start with the easier one; **the flow of current.** The movement of electrons represents the current. As a matter of fact, ever since Franklin assigned the symbols + and – to charge, it was assumed that the movement of charge went from "more" to "less". This movement from positive to negative is called **conventional** flow. We now know that the negative terminal of the battery actually has "more" electrons that are pushed towards the positive terminal, which is missing electrons and is "less". This direction of flow is called **electron** flow. For the purposes of making the explanation easier, we will continue with the electrons moving from – to +.

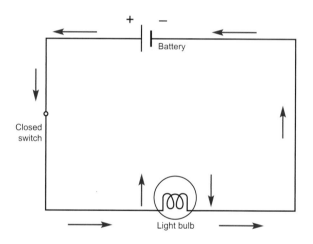

Current flows from – to +. The rate at which the electrons move is important. We must have a method for counting electrons. Suffice it to say that it is impossible to count a quantity of electrons. In the tiniest spark you get from removing your sweater, there are probably 10^{10} electrons zapping around. In a real circuit, you can count on a substantially greater number, for example, 10^{20} (that's not double, that's x 10000000000 times bigger).

When we count eggs and bread rolls, we use dozens. This convenience factor is used in counting electrons but we don't group in 12's. The "group" is 6.25×10^{18} electrons. It isn't important how that number was arrived at because only scientists refer to it. The more common way is to refer to it by its given name – the **Coulomb** (C). The Coulomb measures 6.25×10^{18} electrons. Now, that's only the quantity. Current is the rate at which these electrons flow. A unit that measures the number of Coulombs per second would be more useful. This unit is called an **Ampere** (A). These unit names are in honor of famous scientists. Coulombs count the number of electrons while Amps (the common nickname for the unit) describe the rate of flow. The rate of flow is more correctly called the **current intensity.** This current intensity is given the symbol, I, for use in writing equations.

The equation is as follows:

I = quantity of charge(electrons)/time(seconds)

1 Amp (1 A) is 1 Coulomb/ 1second (1 C/s)

The device that measures current is called an **ammeter.** When it is placed into the circuit so that the current passes through it, the dial is calibrated to show the number of Amps flowing. The meter's placement is critical. It must be positioned so that the entire flow passes through the device. This connection is called series. The ammeter is placed in series with the circuit. In the same way that a water meter must be placed in the flow to measure the rate, the ammeter must be placed in the electron flow.

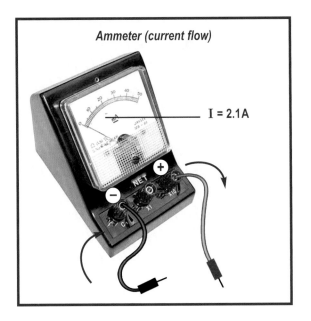

Ammeter (current flow)

I = 2.1A

The energy carried by the current is the second measurement that must be made. This time we are less concerned with the number of electrons that are flowing but with the amount of energy they are carrying and leaving behind. The energy they carry originated at the battery. Back at the battery, the pressure is building up. Each battery has a different "pressure" based on the arrangement of chemicals inside the battery. The unit used to measure this is based on two factors.

The first factor is the total amount of work that can be done on the electrons by the battery and thus that can be delivered to the circuit. The unit for work

(energy) is the Joule (J), (named after James Joule, a Scottish physicist). The second factor is the actual number of electrons being "worked" on. As mentioned before, this unit is the Coulomb (C). Together they express the amount of work (energy) that is stored per unit of charge. This new unit is called voltage and is measured in Volts (V).

Voltage = energy/charge

1 V = 1 J/ 1 C

When describing the battery's potential to deliver electrons and energy, we are referring to the battery's voltage. You are no doubt familiar with the common AA Walkman batteries. These have a voltage of 1.5 V. But so do AAA's, C's and D's. What's the difference? If you've noticed, the D size battery is much larger than the AA. It's the equivalent of having a larger gas tank in your car. You still have the same type of gas and octane only with a larger tank so you can go further. The D size battery will last longer than the AA. It has more electrons ready for use, which explains why it's larger. Its size though makes it less practical for use in portable disc players, for example.

On the other hand, the large 6 V battery used for flashlight lanterns has both more electrons stored inside and more energy per charge. Its larger casing can store more chemicals and more cells can be stacked up to provide the 6 V from the

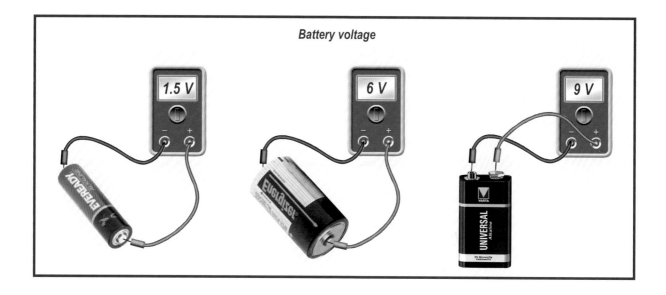

Battery voltage

individual 1.5 V unit cells. This type of battery is not only like having a larger gas tank but also a super charged higher octane gasoline. It would be unwise to think that you could use this 6 V battery to replace a 1.5 V battery. This idea goes back to what the voltage represents. It is the amount of energy that could be delivered by a Coulomb of charge. Six batteries deliver 4 times more energy per Coulomb than the 1.5 V battery. This much extra energy would probably overheat the wiring in your Walkman and fry the circuits. Could you imagine what would happen if you tried one of those 9 V batteries?

Whichever battery you choose, once connected to some wires and a load (a device like a bulb or a radio) and the switch turned on, the current will flow. As the electrons are pushed through the circuit, they give up the energy that they had in the battery. As they move further away from the battery's negative terminal they get closer to the positive terminal. By the time they reach the positive terminal, they are considered grounded. They don't have any more stored energy. But at the positive terminal, they are "worked" on and returned to the negative terminal to start the flow all over again.

This means that along the way the electrons have varying amounts of energy as compared to the original "push". Now, we speak of the potential difference between the amount of energy at the negative terminal and the point at which you wish to measure. The unit for this measurement is the same Volt as before, only now it is referring to the "lost energy" as potential difference. It sounds confusing but think of this voltage as always being a comparison between two parts of the circuit or battery.

The voltage is always measured from one point to another by a voltmeter. This meter must be connected from the first point you wish to check to the second point you wish to observe. It has to be "from the outside". The circuit must be complete and in operation, to be able to measure this drop in potential as the current flows through the circuit. By connecting the voltmeter from one end of the battery to the other, we can measure the total amount of energy delivered per charge to the circuit. On the other hand, by checking the potential from the beginning of the load to the end of the "load", we can see its potential difference. In other words, we can see how much energy it used up.

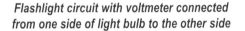

Flashlight circuit with voltmeter connected from one side of light bulb to the other side

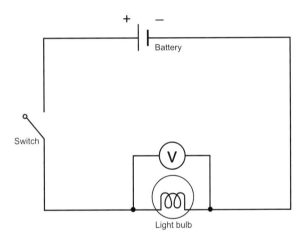

With these two meters in use, the ammeter and the voltmeter, we have both the amount of charge flowing through the circuit per second and the amount of energy used per charge. Together, this will allow us to determine the total amount of energy used by the circuit per second. By multiplying these two values together, we get what is called the **power.** Power is the rate at which a device uses up energy. You've heard of a 100 W light bulb, for instance. Now this can be translated. It means that the light bulb uses energy at a rate

100 J of energy per second while it is turned on. Power is measured in a unit called Watts (W) (named after James Watt, a British physicist), power represents the number of Joules used per second of operation.

Power = energy used/ unit time (second)

1 W = 1 J/ 1 s

Aside from the 100 W light bulb, you've heard of 1000 W microwaves and 200 W speakers. All these describe the power rating for each of these devices. You may wonder as to what is the need for this information. Well, your electrical utility company sells you electricity, right? Wrong, they sell you energy that is delivered by electricity. So, to be able to

charge you for the energy you consume, they use a meter which converts the voltage that is delivered to your house and the amount of current you use into a reading which represents your energy consumption. Now they know how much energy to charge you for.

So in this unit we have seen the setting up of the circuit and all the measurements we can make on it. The meters can be used to determine how much you owe the utility company but in the next section, we'll see how the meters will be used to determine the special laws for circuits.

Notes

_____
_____
_____
_____
_____
_____
_____
_____
_____
_____
_____
_____
_____
_____
_____
_____
_____
_____
_____
_____
_____
_____
_____
_____
_____
_____
_____

Notes

_____
_____
_____
_____
_____
_____
_____
_____
_____
_____
_____
_____
_____
_____
_____
_____

Lesson # 5 – Series Circuits

Objectives:

- Ohm's Law and how to use it.

- The set up of a series circuit.

- The rules for current, voltage, and resistance in the series circuit.

- The use of "the box" to calculate the current, voltage, and resistance in a series circuit.

In a simple circuit, we've seen that a battery will provide the thrust to move electrons through some conducting wires to a device that will use up this energy. A second conducting wire leads the electrons back to the battery to start the process again. With the ammeter and voltmeter, information about the circuit can be gathered. That seems to be the way things work for a simple circuit like a flashlight. There is more to the story than that.

As shown before in a simple circuit, electricity flows through the light. That bulb uses up energy at a rate determined by the type of bulb it is. A 40 W bulb is different from a 100 W bulb. This difference has something to do with the ease or difficulty that the current has in passing through the bulb. This is referred to as the bulb's **resistance** to current flow. If an electrical device has a low resistance, then it allows a relatively large current to pass through it. If it has a high resistance, then a smaller current

would be measured. In mathematical terms, this is an inverse relationship. Resistance (R) is measured in an unusual unit. It is called Ohms and has the Greek symbol, Ω (omega).

There are some devices that are specifically designed to resist the movement of electrons. These devices are called **resistors**. Their function is, of course, to resist. They do so in a very predictable fashion. The larger the battery used, the greater the current flow through the resistor and of course, the smaller the battery the smaller the current. This type of relationship is called **Ohm's Law**. It is the connection between voltage and the current that describes the resistance. One way to write this mathematically is to express it in terms of resistance.

$$R = V/I$$

$$1\ \Omega = 1\ V/\ 1\ A$$

A second more useful way to write this relationship mathematically is to express it in terms of the voltage.

> V = I R   this is the traditional method and it works the best.

A simple circuit contains only one circuit element (one load). In the flashlight, it is the light bulb. Ohm's law would work very nicely with this circuit. For example, a 1.5 V battery might produce a current of 0.1 A. When correctly calculated, the resistance turns out to be 15 Ω.

> V = I R
>
> 1.5 V = (0.1 A) (R)
>
> R = 1.5/0.1
>
> R = 15 Ω

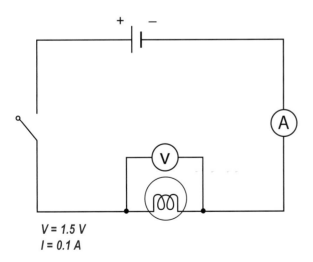

V = 1.5 V
I = 0.1 A

It's time to complicate the circuit. We'll do this by adding extra light bulbs, say two more, to the circuit. It must have an effect on the ease with which current can pass through the new circuit elements. As well, each bulb will use up some of the energy provided by the battery. Some very particular rules will have to be set up to account for the extra bulbs.

By adding extra lights, you could say that it would be like creating a string of Christmas tree lights. The first method for adding on bulbs would be to connect them in sequence, one after the other. Since a bulb has no positive or negative end, it is not crucial which end is connected in sequence to the other. What is most crucial is whether or not you can trace the path of the electrons, beginning at the negative terminal of the battery and ending at the positive terminal of the battery without a break in the circuit. If this can be accomplished, what you have is a series circuit.

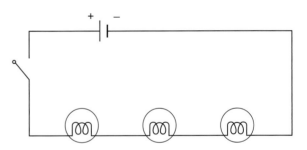

There are three rules to set up for this type of circuit. First, let's consider the use of the voltage (energy). The battery provides all the energy the circuit will have. The bulbs will use this energy up. Each bulb will use some of the total. Since the connecting wires have little or no resistance, they use very little of this energy and we don't have to worry about them. The three light bulbs will split up the energy. They would split it equally if they were all the same strength and type but this may not always be the case. But what will always be true, is that the total of the energy used by each bulb will equal the total energy provided by the battery. Stated mathematically,

$$V_{total} = V_1 + V_2 + V_3$$

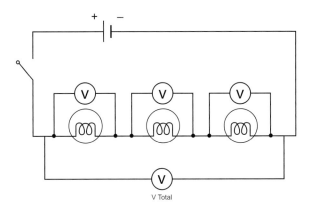

V Total

Remember that we measure the energy used up by a circuit element by the voltage across that element.

This relationship was stated by Kirchoff as his Voltage Law. This law is always true but is most applicable to a series circuit. It is similar to the water of a river dropping through several falls until it reaches bottom. The total height of the falls is the total of the individual falls on the way down.

The second rule deals with the movement of the electrons, the current. In a series circuit, there is only one pathway for the electrons to follow. They leave the negative terminal of the battery, follow the conducting wires to the first light bulb and so on until the pathway is

completed by returning to the positive end of the battery. Just as in a garden hose, the rate at which the water goes into the hose must be matched by the rate of the water leaving the other end. The electrons that leave the battery must come back to it. Therefore, the current that leaves the battery must pass through each and every light bulb. By placing an ammeter at the various locations along the circuit, this can be shown. We simply say that the current is constant throughout the circuit. Stated mathematically,

$$I_{total} = I_1 = I_2 = I_3$$

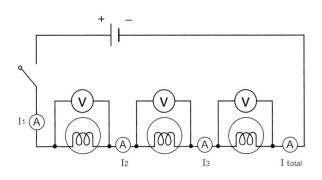

The last rule involves the resistance. Each light bulb has a resistance as determined by its composition (type of metal, etc.). The resistance for each resistor can be determined by using V/I. It would follow then, that if the voltages were added then the resistances should add as well. Does this make sense? Each bulb offers up a resistance to the flow of the current. This is like connecting various sizes (diameters) of hose together end to end and turning on the water. Each hose resists the flow in its own way but they act like one much larger resistance. Stated mathematically,

$$R_{total} = R_1 + R_2 + R_3$$

These three rules apply to any series circuit and could be adapted to take into account more elements connected in a series. At the same time, Ohm's Law is always at work. It applies to the entire circuit.

$$V_{total} = I_{total} \times R_{total}$$

It also applies to each light bulb.

$$V_1 = I_1 \times R_1 \text{ etceteras}$$

Follow this example of a series circuit.

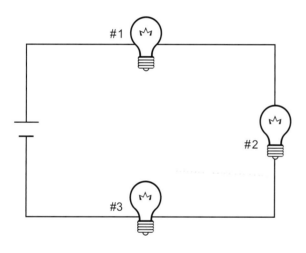

The battery has a voltage of 6 V and the light bulbs have resistances of 10 Ω, 20 Ω and 30 Ω respectively. With this information it is possible to calculate the current, I, of the circuit, as well as the voltage across each light bulb. To do this we must follow the rules. At the same time, we could organize the data so as to make it easier to follow the calculations.

We'll set up a 4 x 3 chart as follows:

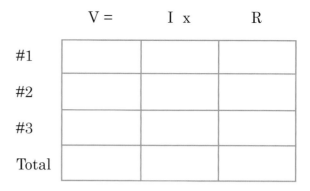

	V =	I x	R
#1			
#2			
#3			
Total			

We can now fill in the given information. That is the V_{total}, and the three resistances.

	V =	I x	R
#1			10 Ω
#2			20 Ω
#3			30 Ω
Total	6 V		

We can start the calculations by using the resistance rule that states that we total up the resistances.

$$R_{total} = R_1 + R_2 + R_3$$

So, 10 + 20 + 30 = 60. Place this in the box.

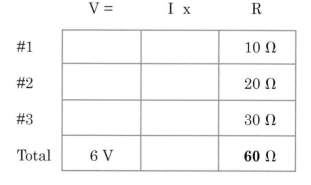

	V =	I x	R
#1			10 Ω
#2			20 Ω
#3			30 Ω
Total	6 V		**60 Ω**

Now, where do we go? The calculation of R_{total} allows us to calculate the value of I_{total}.

$$V_{total} = I_{total} \times R_{total}$$

$6\ V = I_{total} \times 60\ \Omega$

$I_{total} = 0.1\ A$. This value can be placed in the chart.

	V =	I x	R
#1			10 Ω
#2			20 Ω
#3			30 Ω
Total	6 V	**0.1 A**	60 Ω

Our next step is relatively easy. We follow up by using the second rule about current. This states that the current is the same throughout the circuit. That means that we fill this information down the current column of the chart.

	V =	I x	R
#1	**1 V**	0.1 A	10 Ω
#2	**2 V**	0.1 A	20 Ω
#3	**3 V**	0.1 A	30 Ω
Total	6 V	0.1 A	60 Ω

On to our final step.

Finally, we can calculate the individual voltages by again using Ohm's Law. For example,

$V_1 = I_1 \times R_1 = 0.1\ A \times 10\Omega = 1\ V$

We fill in the rest just as easily.

	V =	I x	R
#1	**1 V**	0.1 A	10 Ω
#2	**2 V**	0.1 A	20 Ω
#3	**3 V**	0.1 A	30 Ω
Total	6 V	0.1 A	60 Ω

These values can also be verified by using the appropriate meters. This chart allows us to use the given data to calculate all the missing values in comparative ease. The box almost fills itself in.

That was the easier of the two types of circuits. We'll do the second type of circuit in the next section.

Lesson # 6 - Parallel Circuits

Objectives:

• The set up of a parallel circuit.

• The rules for current, voltage, and resistance in the parallel circuit.

• The use of "the box" to calculate the current, voltage, and resistance in a parallel circuit.

We started with a simple circuit that contained only one light bulb. Then by stringing a few more bulbs in sequence, we created a series circuit. The downside of that circuit is that when one light bulb blows, the whole circuit shuts down. Since electricity can't jump the gap in the broken bulb, the current stops. If car headlights were connected in this series fashion, we'd have serious problems. If one headlight were to blow, it would mean that both would be out. Not a safe way to travel. Since you've seen cars with only one headlight, there must be a second way to connect the light bulbs so that they work independently of each other.

That is the basis for this second arrangement. In fact each light bulb is connected directly to the battery as if the others weren't even there. Take a battery and connect a single light bulb to it. This completes a simple circuit which functions based on Ohm's Law. If a second light bulb is connected to the same battery, it would also work on its own, following Ohm's Law. As long as the battery has enough charge to supply both light bulbs, there is no difficulty with this system. What if we connect a third light bulb? Let's see what this would mean.

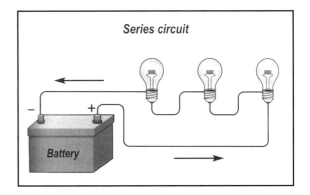

First, since each bulb is connected to the battery, each light bulb would use up all the voltage.

$V_1 = V_{total}$ as would V_2 and also V_3.

This represents the voltage rule for this type of circuit. The name of this circuit is derived from the fact that each light bulb is connected parallel to each other. It is for this reason that it is called a **parallel** circuit. It would be cumbersome to connect each light bulb back to the original battery. There would be far too many wires. A modification was introduced. As long as the light bulb can trace one of its connections back to the negative terminal and the other to the positive end, it does not have to touch the battery directly. That is to say, it can share a connection/pathway with other light bulbs. The three light bulbs have each of the wires from one side of their socket connected together. This branching junction of wires is then connected back to a terminal of the battery using a single wire. The same is done for the wires on the other side of the socket.

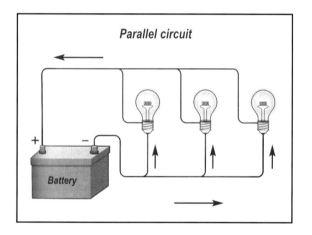

The result is that the electrons leave the negative terminal of the battery and travel along the common connecting wire until the junction. At this point, electrons move along each branch toward the individual light bulbs. Once through the light bulbs, the electrons meet up at the other junction and continue together back to the battery's positive terminal.

Each light bulb gets its own amount of current. This is determined by the light bulb's resistance following Ohm's Law. The greater the resistance, the smaller will be the current. And conversely, for the lower resistance bulb, more current will flow. This describes Kirchoff's second law, as it applies to a parallel circuit's current. "The total current that enters the junction is equal to the total current coming out of it". Stating this mathematically,

$$I_{total} = I_1 + I_2 + I_3$$

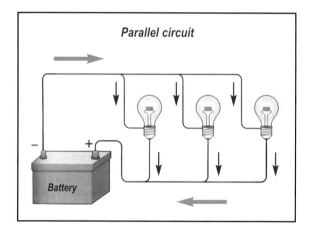

As just explained, all the current leaves the battery, then splits up when it reaches the junction. Each branch containing a light bulb carries its own amount of current. At the second junction, all the current is reunited on its way back to the battery.

The two rules for voltage and current that a parallel circuit follows are different than those for the series circuit. In fact, they are interchanged. It sounded so simple when there was only one circuit type and one set of rules. Now, you'll really have to be able tell the circuits apart. Well, that's going to make it harder to remember. But if you can remember the explanations, then you can always recreate the laws and use them correctly. The last law concerning the resistance is truly different, so read on carefully.

Let's start with the idea that the circuit provides a resistance to the flow of current. The more current that flows through a circuit, the lower the resistance must be in that circuit. Sound right? Then, if the light bulbs can be arranged in a way that allows more current to flow, this would mean that the total resistance of these light bulbs acting together will actually be lower, correct? The idea being, "the more you add, the less you get". How is this possible?

Try this analogy that may put it into the right perspective. A crowd is waiting to get into a concert (no "current" yet). One door opens and people start moving through the turnstile. A rate of flow is established (now, we have current). A second turnstile is opened which obviously increases the flow rate (more pathways, more current). Another turnstile is opened and even though the guard on duty is checking through all the bags, there is still an increase in the number of people that are getting in per time interval (flow rate is increased).

This is the same as in a parallel circuit when an extra light bulb is added on.

Each bulb allows current to pass through itself so that when you total the current for the entire circuit, you will find it has increased. An ammeter would show an increase in the value of the current, I, every time an extra light bulb would be added to the circuit. Since the battery's voltage isn't changing, the increase in current must be due to a decrease in the circuit's total resistance. Somehow, by adding more light bulbs in parallel, it has the effect of lowering the total resistance of the circuit.

It makes sense when we analyze the situation using the concert analogy, but to show this in a mathematical form requires some faith (unless you really want to see the derivation of the next equation). The equation is set up to give a smaller result the more elements you add into the circuit. This is what it looks like when written as an equation.

$$\frac{1}{R_{tot}} = \frac{1}{R_1} + \frac{1}{R_2} + \frac{1}{R_3}$$

In this equation, we are adding the reciprocals of each resistor and our answer is in fact the reciprocal of the total resistance.

It may look like a tough equation but it works. As more light bulbs are added to the circuit/the equation, the total resistance does go down. Let's look at a sample of this with first a simple circuit and then add in the extra light bulbs.

In this circuit, the battery is 6 V and the light bulb has a resistance of 10 Ω. The current would be, according to Ohm's Law,

I = V/R

I = 6 V / 10 Ω = 0.6 A

Now add a 20 Ω light bulb in parallel.

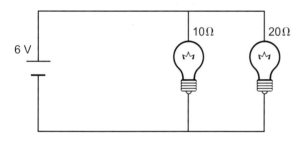

This bulb will draw its own current of

I = 6 V / 20 Ω = 0.3 A

There would be a total current of (0.6 A + 0.3 A) = 0.9 A.

By adding a third light bulb, the current should go even higher. This time let's add a bulb with a higher resistance, say, 60 Ω.

This third light bulb will draw a current of

I = 6 V / 60 Ω = 0.1 A

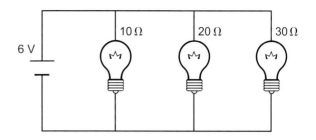

We now have a total of (0.9 A + 0.1 A) = 1.0 A.

Can we get this same answer using the new equation to calculate the total resistance first then I_{total}?

As before,...

$V_{total} = I_{total} \times R_{total}$

By replacing the above data, we have...

$6 V = I_{total} \times ?$

To calculate R_{total}, we must do some math with fractions.

$$\frac{1}{R_{tot}} = \frac{1}{R_1} + \frac{1}{R_2} + \frac{1}{R_3}$$

$$\frac{1}{R_{tot}} = \frac{1}{10\ \Omega} + \frac{1}{20\ \Omega} + \frac{1}{60\ \Omega}$$

As your math teacher taught you, you must find the lowest common denominator. For the three fractions we have here, the lowest common denominator is 60. Each fraction must be converted to a fraction of 60.

$$\frac{1}{R_{tot}} = \frac{6}{60} + \frac{3}{60} + \frac{1}{60} = \frac{10}{60}$$

At this point, we have a total of 10/60. This represents $1/R_{tot}$ which is not exactly what we were looking for but really close. We need R_{tot}. The only way to get it is to flip our answer. This means we now have...

$$\frac{R_{tot}}{1} = \frac{60}{10}$$

$R_{tot} = 6\ \Omega$

We have just calculated the R_{tot} using our new equation. We now go back and solve for the total current.

$6\ V = I_{total} \times 6\ \Omega$

$I_{total} = 1\ A$ just as predicted.

This example can also be calculated using the chart (box) we used for the series circuit but with a modification to take the fractions into account. By adding an extra column and labeling it 1/R, we can keep track of the fractions. Step one, as before is to fill in the given data.

	V =	I x	R	1/R
#1			10 Ω	
#2			20 Ω	
#3			60 Ω	
Total	6 V			

Because it is a parallel circuit, we have to create the reciprocals for each light bulb and place them in the last column, 1/R.

	V =	I x	R	1/R
#1			10 Ω	1/10
#2			20 Ω	1/20
#3			60 Ω	1/60
Total	6 V			

With the reciprocals listed in the chart, we can perform our addition of fractions. As shown above, we calculate the value of fractions to be 10/60 and place this value in the bottom right corner of the chart.

	V =	I x	R	1/R
#1			10 Ω	1/10
#2			20 Ω	1/20
#3			60 Ω	1/60
Total	6 V		←	10/60

To move the value back into the main part of the chart, we flip it over and simplify it as much as possible. We can even just calculate the value on the calculator and include any decimal points (if any). We now have the value for the total resistance.

	V =	I x	R	1/R
#1			10 Ω	1/10
#2			20 Ω	1/20
#3			60 Ω	1/60
Total	6 V		6 Ω ←	10/60

The rest of the chart can be filled in using the special rules that apply only to parallel circuits. We recall that the voltages are the same for each light bulb. This rule allows us to fill 6 V up the Voltage column.

	V =	I x	R	1/R
#1	6 V		10 Ω	1/10
#2	6 V		20 Ω	1/20
#3	6 V		60 Ω	1/60
Total	6 V		6 Ω	10/60

At this stage, each bulb's current can be calculated by using V = IR across each row. (see the finished chart below)

	V =	I x	R	1/R
#1	6 V	0.6 A	10 Ω	1/10
#2	6 V	0.3 A	20 Ω	1/20
#3	6 V	0.1 A	60 Ω	1/60
Total	6 V	1.0 A	6 Ω	10/60

To confirm that everything has worked out according to plan, we can verify the current rule. By adding the individual currents together, if no mistakes were made along the way the total should be 1.0 A.

Phew! That parallel circuit seems to have a few more steps in the calculations as compared to a series circuit but the rationale for the circuit makes sense. A new set of rules which are similar to but different from those of series are,

- voltages are the same

- current values add up to the total current

- resistance must be added by using reciprocals (1/R)

- Ohm's Law still applies to each resistor and to the total values.

The parallel circuit's set up allows for more applications than the series circuit. This type of circuit is the one used for your car's headlights. When one headlight goes out, the other one is still on because it has its own circuit to the battery. It's not only your car that has this type of circuitry, but your house as well. We'll save that discussion for the next section.

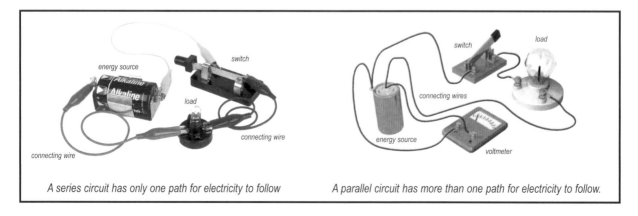

A series circuit has only one path for electricity to follow   A parallel circuit has more than one path for electricity to follow.

Lesson # 7 – In the Home

Objectives:

- The type of circuit used to wire a home.

- The difference between DC and AC electricity.

- The set up of a home's electrical entry panel.

- Grounding electrical outlets.

As you've already seen, we have two main types of circuits – series and parallel. It would seem that series is simpler and probably cheaper but not as practical as parallel.

Houses are wired in a way that allows you to use each light or appliance on its own. Turning on the stereo requires its own switch. If you turn on the lights, they have no effect on the stereo. There is no need to turn on the microwave just so the juicer will work. Each appliance and light generally works on its own, as with the 3 light bulbs that were connected to the battery individually. This is the parallel set up.

You may find though that when you plug in a hair dryer, microwave, toaster oven, and turn on the lights in the kitchen at the same time that they may all suddenly stop working. Guess what? This also shows that your house is wired in parallel.

The more pathways, the more total current. All those appliances turned on at once would certainly represent more current. The more current flowing, the more heat that the wires carrying the current build up. Recall that conducting wires take away very little energy from the electrons. This is true for small currents but the amount described above would be enough to cause a fire. There is a safety factor that must be considered.

The wires conducting the electricity throughout your house are in the walls. If those wires were to overheat, they could ignite the wood in the walls. It is for this reason that engineers have designed a special entry panel for the control of electricity in the home.

The electricity that comes into your house is generated in a different way than that of the batteries we've been using. Batteries have a negative and positive terminal and thus have a **direct**

current from the negative to the positive. The electricity that arrives by high-tension lines to your home is an **alternating current**. The electrons move back and forth very quickly. As they do, this "push and pull" gives the electrons energy that they deliver to your stereo, etc.

The typical set up is that there are three wires leading into the house. One wire is the **neutral**, or grounded, wire. This wire is connected to the base of the panel and to the box containing all the wiring. The box, in turn, is grounded to the plumbing of the house and/or directly into the ground. As you recall, this eliminates excess charge which can build up anywhere in the circuitry and cause shocks and sparks.

The other two wires carry 120 V each. These "hot" wires pass through a meter that will measure the amount of electrical energy that you use. The meter is usually placed outside for easier reading. The two 120 V conducting wires then pass through a switch box. This has a master switch that allows you to cut the power to the entire house. This is particularly useful when major rewiring has to be done in the house. Each wire is connected in series with a fuse or circuit breaker. The fuse is a device that has a strip of metal inside for the electricity to flow through. If too much electricity

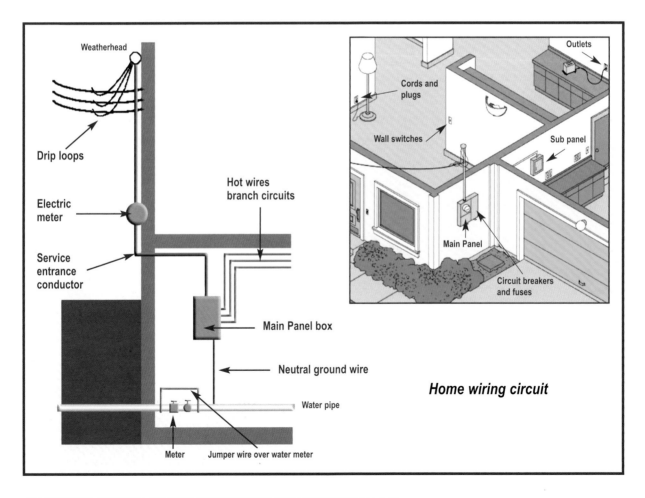

Home wiring circuit

passes through, the wire will overheat and melt. Since this is a series circuit, when the wire snaps it stops the current for the rest of the circuit, probably avoiding a fire in the process.

All three conducting wires are then connected to a panel. From this panel, all the circuits to service the house will be taken and branched off. When a branch circuit is set up, a connection is made to the neutral wire and either one

of the 120 V wires. A circuit breaker works like the fuse except that a spring mechanism flips a shut off switch. This is connected in series to the "hot" wire. Light sockets and outlet sockets will be placed along the length of this branch wire. All these are connected in parallel so that they can work independently. Light switches are connected in series with the light they are to control.

You may have noticed that wall outlets have three holes for each plug, one almost round hole and two different sized slots. This type of outlet is said to be polarized. The narrow slot is always connected to the 120 V wire (black) whereas the larger slot is connected to the neutral (white) wire. This is coordinated with the new appliances that have the corresponding plugs. They are connected in this fashion so that the "live" wire is connected in series with the switch of the appliance or lamp. In this way electricity can't "leak" into the device and cause a shock.

The grounding pin is also an important part of the outlet. It is connected back to the panel and to the main ground of the house. When an appliance is plugged in, the ground of the plug is connecting the outside casing of the appliance to the ground. If any current would jump across a faulty connection, it would follow a path back to the ground and pass through the person holding the device. The ground wire removes this possibility.

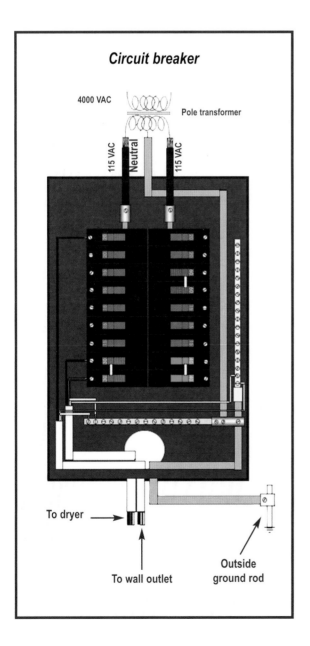

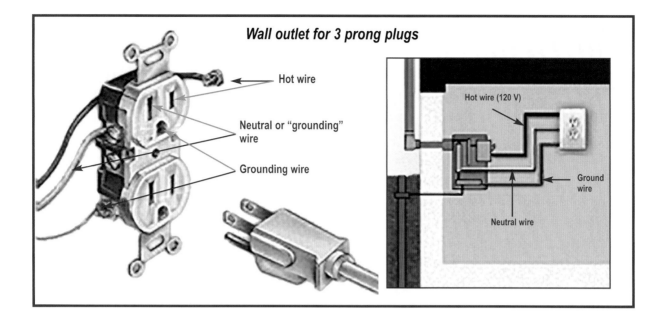

Wall outlet for 3 prong plugs

Hot wire

Neutral or "grounding" wire

Grounding wire

Hot wire (120 V)

Ground wire

Neutral wire

As many as twenty-four 120 V branches are typically connected to a distribution panel. As you recall, the thicker the wire, the more current it can carry. This is true in setting up the wiring for the house. Depending on the thickness of wire used for a circuit, a circuit breaker may be set to withstand anywhere from 20 A to 30 A, for example. Any of these safety features have been well thought out and should not be changed.

Some appliances though require more energy than can be provided by the 120 V lines. For these cases, the two 120 V lines are used to create a special 240 V circuit. Dryers, ovens, and air conditioning units are examples of devices that would need to draw more power. They also tend to have special circuit breakers that allow for the increased current drawn by the appliance.

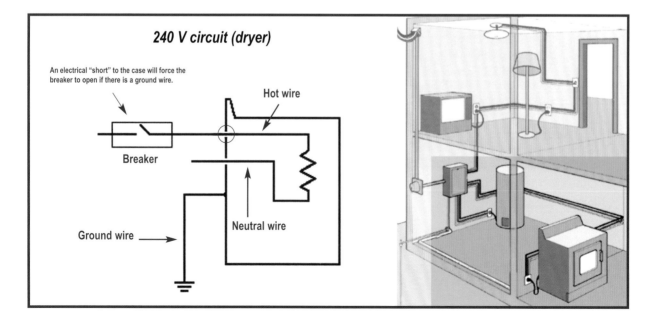

240 V circuit (dryer)

An electrical "short" to the case will force the breaker to open if there is a ground wire.

Hot wire

Breaker

Ground wire

Neutral wire

Since all the electricity coming to the house passes through the meter, the utility company always has an accurate record of the amount of electrical energy you use.

Whether you use a 120 V connected light bulb or a 240 V connected oven, you are using energy derived from the movement of electrons.

So, it does in fact go back to the structure of the atom and our ability to harness its energy.

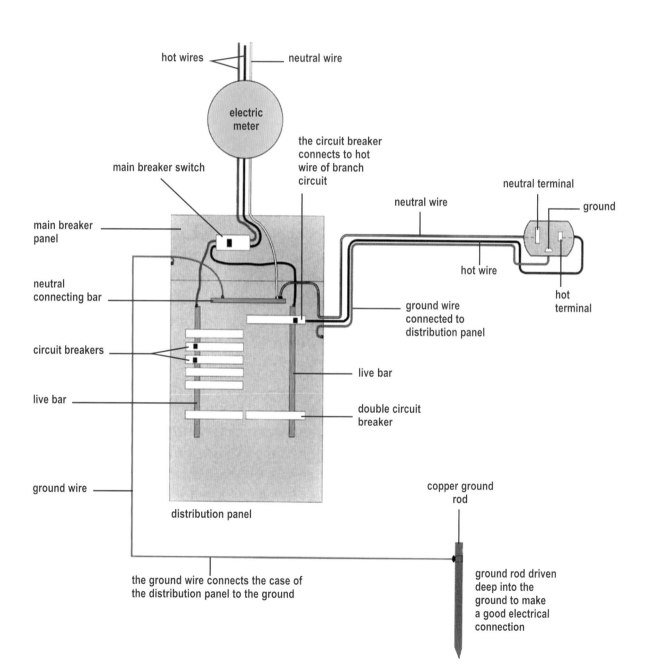

hot wires — neutral wire

electric meter

main breaker switch

the circuit breaker connects to hot wire of branch circuit

neutral terminal

ground

neutral wire

main breaker panel

hot wire

neutral connecting bar

ground wire connected to distribution panel

hot terminal

circuit breakers

live bar

live bar

double circuit breaker

ground wire

copper ground rod

distribution panel

the ground wire connects the case of the distribution panel to the ground

ground rod driven deep into the ground to make a good electrical connection

Unit 1 – Questions

Were You Paying Attention?

By now, you've read all the previous sections. You've heard a lot about electrons and how they carry energy. You've learned about series & parallel circuits and even how your house is wired. With all that information, you should be able to do these few review questions.

1. Who was the first scientist to restate Democritus' idea of the "indestructible" atom?

_____

2. When objects are charged with static electricity, what are the two possible results of bringing two of these objects close together? Why?

_____

_____

3. Name two types of electroscopes.

_____

4. What do a battery and a generator do to provide the conditions for electricity to flow?

_____

5. Name at least one other way of producing the potential for an electric current.

_____

6. What are the three essential components for a simple circuit?

_____

7. Name the two types of meters & state what each measures.

_____

8. State the rules in a series circuit for   a) voltage   b) resistance.

_____

_____

9. Complete "the box" for a series circuit.

	V =	I x	R
#1			10 Ω
#2			20 Ω
Total		2 A	

10. State the rules in a parallel circuit for   a) voltage   b) current

_____

_____

_____

_____

11. Complete "the box" for a parallel circuit.

	V =	I x	R
#1		2 A	
#2			
Total	30 V		10 R

12. What type of circuit is the main one used for home wiring?

_____

13. What is the main safety feature built into electrical entry panels to protect against overloads?

_____

SIMPLE MACHINES: FORCE AND WORK

Simple Machines: Force and Work

Introduction

You pick up a book and carry it over to the bookcase. You place it on the shelf. You go back to your seat and pick up a nutcracker and crack yourself a few walnuts. You start feeling guilty about all the work you haven't done yet.

Outside, you see the earth that was moved by a power shovel just waiting for you. Using your shovel, you load up the wheelbarrow and move the earth up the ramp to the top of the mound.

The roofer yells down to you that he'd like your help by putting some shingles on the palette so that they can be raised by using the block and tackle system he's rigged up. Meanwhile, you'd prefer that he help you move some rocks by using a large crowbar. Since some of these rocks are too large, you use a chisel to split them by hitting them with a sledgehammer.

To make certain that the rocks don't shift, you turn on the tap and use the hose to spray the walkway by squeezing the pistol on the garden hose.

You screw together some 2"x4's. The frame seems to be holding in the rocks well.

You've built up a thirst so you pop the top of a can of soda. That feels good! Time to go inside for a well earned nap.

Back in your den, the sun's too bright so you pull on the cord to let down the blind. You go over to the radio and turn the volume knobs to crank out the latest music. By turning another knob, you dim the lights in the room. You plop down in your recliner and pull the lever. The footrest pops out and all is well with the world.

As you drift off to sleep, you think about going to the local hardware store to pick up a few new machines to help you do the work around the house. If only you'd had some machines while you were doing today's work. Well, in fact, you did only you didn't realize it.

Actually, you were surrounded by simple machines. Simple machines were there when you turned the volume knob of the radio. A simple machine was there as the chisel split the rock. What about when you screwed the 2"x4"s together. That was also a simple machine. No need for power tools to feel that machines are at work. Simple machines are everywhere, and they help you do work.

All that work you did was aided by the use of simple machines. Each machine had its own way in which it took your work and made it its work. In this section, you will learn about what work really is and then how simple machines take this work and modify it. Each machine's transformation of this work is controlled by special rules and equations. So, get your calculator and pencil ready as we delve into the rules that govern work and machines.

Simple Machines

Power Tools

Lesson # 1 – How to Get to Work

Objectives:

- The true meaning of work (physics style).

- The definition of force.

- The meaning of the force of gravity (weight).

- The equation for doing work.

It's time to roll up our sleeves and get down to work. The only problem is that you and I will disagree on what the word work actually means.

You probably have the idea that work is something you get paid for or something you don't want to do but have to. Sorry, but work has a special definition in physics that depends upon force and displacement. Let's examine the two components of work; force and displacement.

A force is a push or pull. A force can either push something or be used to pull something. A push or a pull must have a direction associated with it. Can you imagine pushing on something without pushing in some direction? Impossible. True, an object can have several forces acting on it in more than one direction but each force has its own direction.

This concept of direction is important in Physics and will show up in machines as well.

To represent forces on paper, vector diagrams are used. A vector is drawn as an arrow with the head pointing in the direction of the force and the tail indicating the location where the force is applied. A dot is often used to represent the point of application of force. When drawing a vector you must first select a scale, as the length of the arrow represents the magnitude of the force.

There are several methods for designating direction:

The first method uses a graphical coordinate system with map convention: North/top, South/bottom, East/right, West/left. Suppose you let 1-centimeter represent 10 units of force. A force of 50 units applied at 30° North-of-East could be represented by drawing a 5-centimeter line segment 30° North of a line drawn to the East. See below.

The second method uses a cartesian plane and degrees. Using as a reference a line drawn to the East, the angle is usually measured counter clockwise.

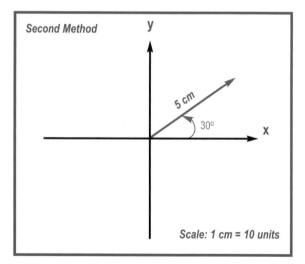

The angle can be as little as 0°, which really means pointing east, to as much as 360° which is when you've come full

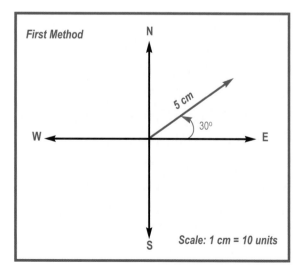

circle and are pointing to East again. For our purposes, we will use an even simpler technique, using left/right and up/down arrows to show the direction of the force vectors.

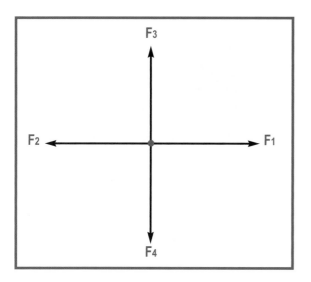

So, we have a force pushing or pulling in a designated direction. Since we have ways to represent our direction, we now need a way to measure our force. The standard unit in Physics is the unit called the Newton. This is in honor of

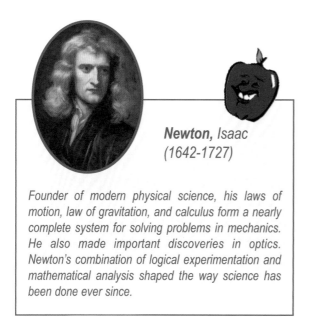

Newton, *Isaac*
(1642-1727)

Founder of modern physical science, his laws of motion, law of gravitation, and calculus form a nearly complete system for solving problems in mechanics. He also made important discoveries in optics. Newton's combination of logical experimentation and mathematical analysis shaped the way science has been done ever since.

Sir Isaac Newton and does have a bit to do with his observation of a falling apple. He observed that the apple was being pulled downward towards the earth. He went on to speculate about how the sun may pull the earth, and other heavenly bodies, but our concern is the pull on that apple.

1N force due to gravity

1N force due to gravity

It turns out that the strength of the earth's pull on an average apple is actually one Newton, written as 1N. The way we calculate the magnitude (that's how we say <u>strength</u> in "Physics talk") of a force is based on a simple equation. We'll just touch on it briefly so that we can use the proper format for our forces.

Our definition of a force's push or pull can be expanded. It can be said that a force has the ability to make an object move. More so, it can make it go faster, or accelerate. This is stated in equation form as follows.

$F = ma$

In other words, this states that a force can take an object that has mass, m, and accelerate it at a rate of "a". But, it's true that not all forces actually cause masses to move, it's just that they have the potential to cause movement. The earth's force, usually referred to as the force of gravity, F_g, acts on all objects and is always trying to move them towards the earth's surface. The strength it pulls on each object is determined by the object's mass, which in our scientific unit system has to be in kilograms, kg. The second part of F_g's equation is more complex but suffice it to say that the acceleration each object would get if air resistance were eliminated would be the same.

Going back to our equation of

$F = ma$

We can now adapt this to deal with the force of gravity, F_g.

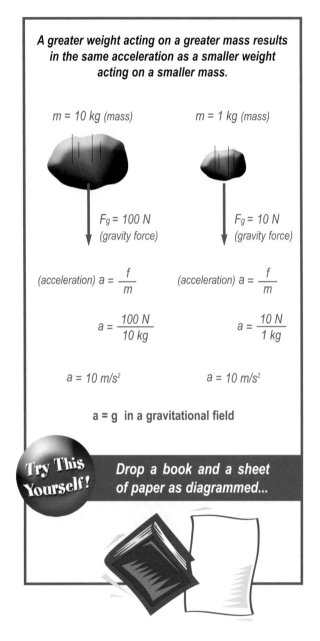

A greater weight acting on a greater mass results in the same acceleration as a smaller weight acting on a smaller mass.

m = 10 kg (mass)   m = 1 kg (mass)

$F_g = 100\ N$ (gravity force) $F_g = 10\ N$ (gravity force)

(acceleration) $a = \dfrac{f}{m}$ (acceleration) $a = \dfrac{f}{m}$

$a = \dfrac{100\ N}{10\ kg}$ $a = \dfrac{10\ N}{1\ kg}$

$a = 10\ m/s^2$ $a = 10\ m/s^2$

a = g in a gravitational field

Try This Yourself!   **Drop a book and a sheet of paper as diagrammed...**

We say that the F_g is equal to the object's mass (in kg) multiplied by the acceleration that is caused by gravity. We use a small "g" to represent this value. In equation form, it looks like this,

$F_g = mg$

First off, the value of "g" is almost the same everywhere in the world. Most physics teachers approximate it at $9.8m/s^2$. (m/s^2 means meters per second squared and describes the rate of acceleration.) Other physics teachers like going one step further and rounding off this value to $10m/s^2$.

We can now calculate the strength of the earth's gravitational force on Newton's apple. The standard apple is about 100 grams. This is another standard unit to represent mass. In fact, we really have to change this unit to kilograms to use it in our force equation. To do that, we divide our number of grams by 1000 (kilo=1000).

$$\frac{100 \text{ grams}}{1000} = 0.1 \text{ kilogram (0.1 kg)}$$

With our mass stated in the correct units, we can calculate the force of gravity acting on it.

$$F_g = mg$$

$$F_g = (0.1 \text{ kg}) (10m/s^2)$$

$$F_g = 1 \text{ kg } m/s^2$$

Now, we simplify the units by exchanging the "kg.m/s²" for "N"

$$F_g = 1N$$

Now, we know the "weight" (that's our nickname for the force of gravity acting on an object) of a 100g apple.

This gives us a picture of a force (push or pull) and a sense for its magnitude (strength). When we get to machines, we'll see how F_g fits in. Sometimes, we can rely on gravity to do our work for us. In most instances though, we will have to be the ones to apply the force. Our effort will go into the machine and show up somewhere else as output.

We still have one more component to our work formula. We have the force pushing in a pre-determined direction but what we don't have yet is the movement. Only when the force causes the object to move will we have work done. When no movement, or more precisely, no displacement has occurred we have no work done. This certainly sounds like an equation. The equation for work is in fact, very simple. For our purposes, we'll keep things moving together, in the same direction, that is. This avoids lots of calculations involving direction. The equation relates the force to the movement as follows.

$$\text{work} = \text{force x distance}$$
$$w = F \ d$$

Looks simple.

It does have some restrictions though. Force, of course, has to be expressed in N. The "d" has to represent a displacement, a movement from one place to another in a specific direction. It must be measured in meters. Only one direction at a time is allowed. And finally, the force has to be in the same

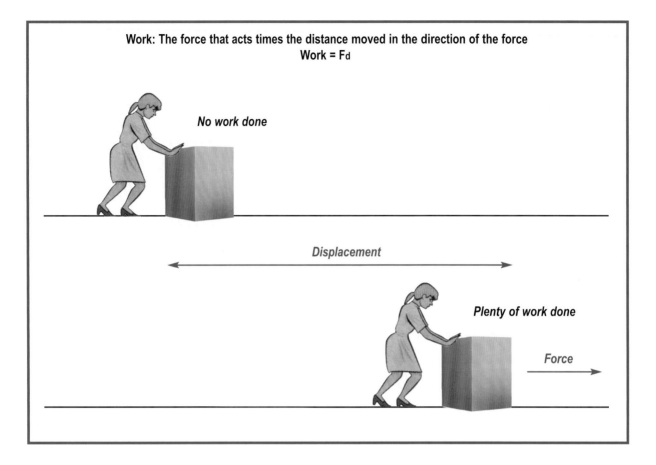

Work: The force that acts times the distance moved in the direction of the force
Work = Fd

No work done

Displacement

Plenty of work done

Force

direction as the movement. In the next section, you'll practice some of these important calculations.

To wrap up this introduction to work, we're going to simplify one more thing. In physics, units tend to get piled up with each other (look at accelerations with its m/s²). Anyway, work being equal to two measured units being multiplied together has been abbreviated to a more universal unit.

N x m *becomes* Joule (J)

To replace our Newton x meter, we have the new unit called Joule. We'll use the initial, J, to represent this as we tackle work problems in our next section.

Joules, *James Prescott (1818-1889)*

English physicist. His scientific researches began in his youth when he invented an electromagnetic engine. Joule made valuable contributions to the fields of heat, electricity, and thermodynamics. His work established the mechanical theory of heat, and he was the first to determine the relationship between heat energy and mechanical energy (the mechanical equivalent of heat). Joule discovered the first law of thermodynamics, which is a form of the law of conservation of energy. He was one of the great experimental scientists of the 19th century. The mechanical unit of work is named for him.

Lesson # 2 – The Problem with Work

Objectives:

- The applied force, F_a.

- The amount of work done against friction.

- The work done to lift an object.

As we've seen, to do work requires a variety of factors to come together.

1. a force has to be applied (force, F)

2. the object has to move (displacement, d)

3. some portion of the force has to be in the direction that the object moves.

Once these three conditions are put together, we can then calculate the amount of work done. The equation we are using is

$$\text{work} = Fd$$

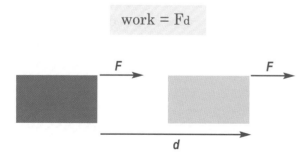

To simplify the equation, we refer to the amount of force pushing or pulling in the direction of motion, this way we avoid complicated trigonometry.

You may be wondering how a force can move an object yet not be acting in the same direction as the movement. Well, it's actually simple. It happens all the time. Suppose you're walking through the airport pulling your suitcase along on its wheels. Look closely; you're not pulling in the same direction as the motion. Your force is in a diagonal direction yet the suitcase moves horizontally. It really doesn't seem right to multiply your full force with the displacement of the suitcase to get the work done.

movement

If you were to pull strictly horizontally, then the full value of your force would be applied through the suitcase's displacement. In this way, you'd be getting full value for your work. However, your back couldn't take it, so you stand up and pull on the handle. The handle makes an angle to the floor and in so doing reduces the effectiveness of your applied force, F_a.

Some of the F_a is directed horizontally

Only a portion of its strength is used in the horizontal direction. It takes the use of a special equation from trigonometry to calculate the appropriate amount. To keep things moving along smoothly, we'll try to stick to situations where the angle has no effect. So, back to work.

Let's try several examples to make certain that we've got the idea down pat.

Question 1

A 10N force pulls horizontally on a 2 kg object. It moves the object 4m across the floor. How much work was done?

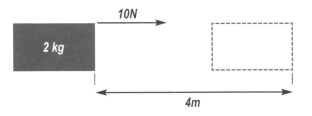

To answer any type of physics problem, you should always follow some basic rules.

First, you must read the question thoroughly to establish what the problem is all about. Once you've decided that the question makes sense, you reread the question but this time extract each bit of information, specifically numerical values, by making a list of the given information. In the given example, upon rereading it, you should have a list as follows.

$F = 10N$ (the applied force, F_a)
$m = 2kg$ (mass of object moved)
$m = 4m$ (distance object moved)

In the question, it seems that the force is in the same direction as the motion since nothing to the contrary is mentioned (see diagram). So on to work.

Therefore,   work = Fd
work = (10N) (4m)
work = 40 N-m

Which, because a $\quad$ N-m = J

becomes $\quad$ work = 40J

But what about the 2 kg mass of the box? It seems we didn't have to take it into account. Mass, it has no direction. The earth's gravitational force, which acts on the mass, does pull on it but only in a downward direction. It would seem that the floor is strong enough to support the weight of the object so that our horizontally applied force works along the distance of the 4m movement.

You know what probably did happen though. The force of gravity pulling down on the object probably set up some friction and that's what our work was doing, overcoming friction. By our calculation, 40J of work was done against friction as the object was moved. Let's try another working situation.

Question 2

It seems that 120J of work was needed to move a crate 3m across the floor. What was the force needed to do "the job"?

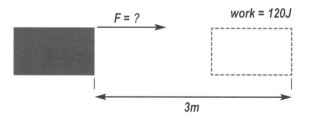

Again, read, reread and make the list.

work = 120J

d = 3m

This time we're looking for the force. First, replace the number values in the equation and then do algebraic steps to get the final answer.

Work = F$_d$

120J = (F) (3m)

divide both sides by 3m

$$\frac{120J}{3m} = \frac{(F)\ (3m)}{3m}$$ $\quad$ 3m is now gone from this side

$$\frac{40J}{m} = F$$

Our last step is to solve for the units. Since a J is really a N-m, we have

$$\frac{40\ N\text{-}m}{m} = F$$

Finally, $\quad$ F = 40N

The next question involves a different look.

Question 3

A 4 kg bag of sugar on the floor has to be placed on a shelf 1.5m high. How much work is done in lifting up the bag of sugar?

According to the information given, we have only two amounts.

m = 4.kg

and height = 1.5m

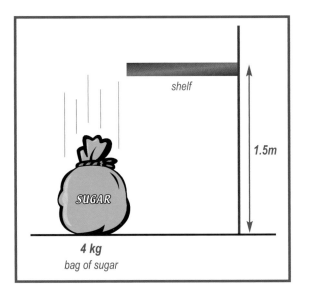

So on the average, we use a 40N force bottom to top.

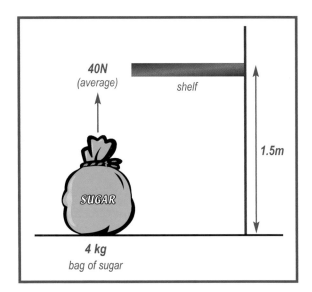

Neither of these are "F" nor "d", or are they?

First, the mass. To lift an object, we have to apply a force upwards with at least as much force as gravity pulls downward. Recall that the pull of gravity has its own equation.

$F_g = mg$ (g = 10m/s² for our purpose)

In this example, the object's weight (F_g) is:

$F_g = (4 \text{ kg}) (10\text{m/s}^2)$
$= (40\text{N})$

This tells us that to lift the bag upwards we must apply a force of at least 40N to raise it up.

The truth is we need a tiny bit more than 40N to get it started but only 40N to continue moving it. At the top, our force will actually be a tiny bit less than 40N, the slowing down part of the movement.

To finish off the question, the distance that our 40N force acts is actually the height to the shelf. The calculation becomes quite easy now.

work = Fd

F = 40N, as described above
d = 1.5m, the height of the
    shelf from the floor

work = (40N) (1.5m)
    = 60 N-m
work = 60J

But, say we complicate this a little by moving the bag of sugar to a higher shelf, say 50cm higher. Now, it will be at a height of 1.5m + 50cm.

Let's fix that right now.

100cm = 1m

So, 50cm = 1/2m or 0.5m

Therefore, its height is now
1.5m + 0.5m = 2m

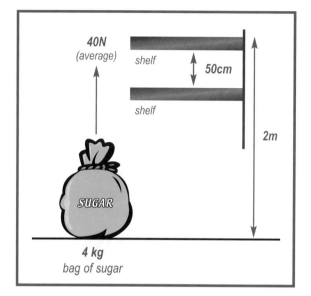

40N
(average)

shelf

50cm

shelf

2m

SUGAR

4 kg
bag of sugar

To move the sugar the extra height, we would do extra work.

work = Fd

work = (40N) (0.5m)
= 20N.m
work = 20J

In total, we did

work = 60J + 20J
= 80J

Is this the same as if we had lifted the bag directly up to the 2m high shelf?

Let's check it out.

The force needed is still 40N but the height is now 2.0m

work = Fd

work = (40N) (2.0m)
= (80N.m)
work = 80J

It looks like it doesn't matter whether we did the "job" in two steps or all at once. The work done is determined by the final job completed.

The job of lifting objects has been with us since time began. Some of the work done by early man has been astounding. Think of just a few examples that boggle the imagination.

Stonehenge

Easter Island
Statues

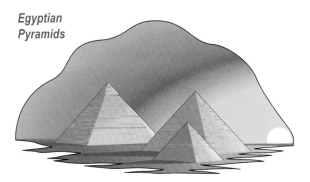

Egyptian Pyramids

How could those large stones have been moved and lifted? It was tough enough working in the backyard. But didn't you have help in that department? The chisel, the wheelbarrow, the block and tackle set-up. They all use force to help you do a job. They don't have any motors or electrical connections. They're just <u>simple machines</u>.

Somehow, early man must have found a way to help himself do the job. Brute force wasn't enough to create these structures. And do you think it was much different when all those amazing churches were being built? Again, there were no engines or motors to drive the bulldozer or operate a crane. The work had to be done by applying a force over a distance but with the help of <u>simple machines</u>.

Now that we have the most basic concept of what work is, we can go on to explore the three basic types of machines. How the work we put into the machine comes out "the other end". As you will see, there is no guarantee that it will be easier using the machine but there will probably be some advantage. So let's check out <u>simple machines</u>.

Lesson # 3 – Getting the Machine to Do the Work

Objectives:

• Work input versus work output.

• The meaning of F_e, d_e, F_r and d_r.

• The difference between AMA and IMA.

To do work, we need to apply a force, which moves an object over a distance. To keep the complications to a minimum, we'll only consider applying the force in the same direction as the movement. In this way, we can describe distances more easily and avoid all that trigonometry stuff.

We, next, have to define the job that needs to be done. To keep all our different machines working together properly, we'll limit ourselves to one basic job.

THE JOB: This will be to lift a 1 kg object 1m off the ground. Each machine will get its chance to do the job so that we can compare how each takes our force and re-uses it.

The first way to do the job would be to lift it ourselves. How much work would that be? Let's figure that out.

The mass we need to lift is 1 kg. That means that gravity is pulling downwards with a force equal to...

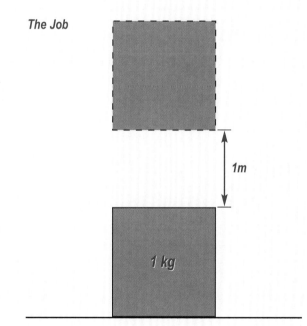

The Job

1m

1 kg

$$F_g = mg$$
$$= (1\ kg)\ 10m/s^2$$
$$= 10N$$

That's right! 10N.

To lift the object, we have to exert a 10N force (on the average). Hopefully, we have enough strength to apply that much force.

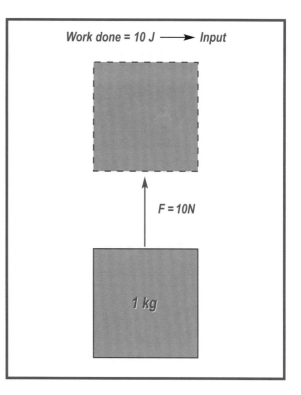

Work done = 10 J → Input

F = 10N

1 kg

Now, for the work part. Our force will be 10N while the distance will be only 1m.

So, how much work is that?

Recall,

work = (F) (d)
So, the work we put in is
work = (10N) (1m)
= 10N-m
since 1N-m = 1J
work = 10J

Thus, we put in 10J of work to lift the object. It now has 10J of work done on it. It's stored "in" the object's position in case we want 10J of energy.

How is that? Well, if we attach a rope to the object and put that over a pulley and then let it "fall" down, it can do work for us as an "output".

We put work in, which can turn into work output at a later time. Actually, it

is usually said that the object resists us putting work into it (the lifting). That is true because gravity is pulling down on the object as we are trying to lift it up. As we are lifting it 1m over the entire distance, our input is being resisted. It can be said that gravity is doing work against us. How about that! You put work in and gravity works against you.

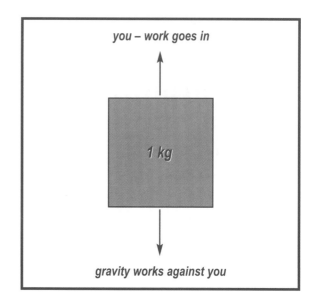

you – work goes in

1 kg

gravity works against you

Well, that's the way it works. You supply the muscle power to put work into a lifting, moving job and gravity resists your efforts. Your effort force (it's really called that and is represented by the symbol, F_e) is countered by a resisting force of gravity (which goes by the symbol, F_r). As you move the object along a distance that you apply your effort, the distance is termed the effort distance, d_e.

Because gravity is acting against you all the way, the force is termed the resistance force, F_r and the distance through which it resists you is termed the resistance distance, d_r.

Your work is being matched by a second amount of work. It is officially represented as:

$$\text{work input} = \text{work output}$$

Your effort is termed as <u>input</u>, with your force being F_e and your distance being, d_e.

Meanwhile, the object's final "resting place" represents the job done, work output. It comes from the force of gravity resisting the "job" over that distance it was moved. We then have an "F_r" to counter your "F_e" and a "d_r" to counter your "d_e"

Since any type of work is based on the equation
$$\text{work} = (F)\ (d)$$
Then your input work is expressed as
$$\text{work input} = (F_e)\ (d_e)$$
And correspondingly, gravity's work is expressed as
$$\text{work output} = (F_r)\ (d_r)$$

Thus far, we've said that to lift a 1 kg object 1m requires 10J of input work. It now means that we have 10J of output work represented by gravity's, F_r (which is equal to the object's weight) acting over that same 1m distance.

Where does that leave us?

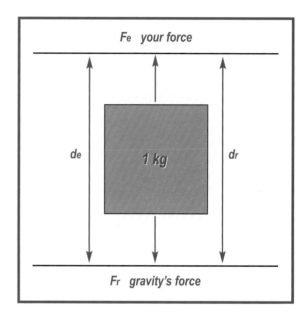

We put in 10J of work.
We get out 10J of work.
$$\text{work input} = \text{work output}$$

We can go one step further and use the (F) (d) equations and rewrite this as

$$(F_e)\ (d_e) = (F_r)\ (d_r)$$

Remember, we're trying to keep this as simple as possible so we are going to assume that in all cases, what we put in is what we get out.

Under these conditions, the equation

(Fe) (de) = (Fr) (dr)

is totally valid. "What goes in must come out." We now have the fundamentals to explore the deeper truths about doing work.

In our example, our effort, F_e, has been matched, Newton for Newton, by gravity's resisting force, F_r. There doesn't seem to be much advantage to this arrangement. Actually, that is very true. There is no actual advantage to doing the job this way. If we were to compare our force to gravity's as a fraction,

$$\frac{F_r}{F_e}$$

There would be nothing special that would indicate any advantage at all, since it equals one.

In reality, this fraction has a name. It's called the Actual Mechanical Advantage.

AMA, for short.

$$AMA = \frac{\text{resistance force}}{\text{effort force}}$$

$$AMA = \frac{F_r}{F_e}$$

In our example of lifting an object straight up

$$F_e = F_r$$

Actual Mechanical Advantage
AMA = 1

$$\text{Therefore,} \quad AMA = F_r$$
$$= \frac{F_e}{1N}$$
$$= \frac{1N}{1}$$

Hence, our way of doing the work has an advantage of 1. That doesn't seems like any Advantage at all.

That's partly correct. An AMA = 1 tells us that whatever F_r awaits us; we have to supply a force of equal value.

AMA also has the word mechanical in it. This refers to some type of machine. You doing the lifting means that you are the machine. So, when you do the lifting directly, you get no mechanical advantage.

You could have seen that coming because you lifted the object 1m and it in fact, moved 1m. Your distance matched that of the object. It turns out that the ratio of your distance, de, to that of the object, dr, also represents a type of advantage.

Couldn't tell that from the numbers, could you?

This advantage is called the Ideal Mechanical Advantage, IMA. It allows us to predict the advantage we're going to get before we do the job.

In this case, the IMA is

$$IMA = \frac{\text{effort distance}}{\text{resistance distance}}$$

$$IMA = \frac{d_e}{d_r}$$

and since $d_e = d_r$

$$IMA = 1$$

Ideal Mechanical Advantage
IMA = 1

$d_e = d_r$

Again, we are being told that there is no extra advantage to doing this job by ourselves. In both cases, AMA and IMA turn out to be 1. It corresponds to the "what we put in, is what we get out" idea. That is partly true. But before we bring in machines to help us do the job,

let's wrap up this discussion with a quick comparison of AMA and IMA.

The AMA ratio involves your part in doing the work. You are the source of the F_e. You want your F_e to be used to its fullest capacity. In the example, we have not included any possibility of wasting some of your force. In real life, there is almost always some force, like friction, that makes you exert more force than is "actually" needed. That's why this ratio,

$$AMA = \frac{F_r}{F_e}$$

is called the <u>actual</u> mechanical advantage. When we "actually" do the work, we may have to exert a greater F_e and thus have a lower than 1 advantage.

On the other hand, when we check out the distances involved, there is nothing to alter them. The distances are simply measurements of where movement will occur. We measure d_e, measure d_r and that's it! No outside factors will change these values.

Recall, we are still talking about lifting our 1 kg object straight up to a height of 1m. All our discussion centers on these basic principles.

1. work input = $(F_e)(d_e)$
2. work output = $(F_r)(d_r)$
3. work input = work output
4. $IMA = \frac{d_e}{d_r}$
5. $AMA = \frac{F_r}{F_e}$

In our "lifting" scenario, we don't seem to get any break, no extra advantage. That is true, that's why we have simple machines. In the next few sections, we will see how simple machines can work to our advantage.

Lesson # 4 – Off to the Playground

Objectives:

- A playground is full of simple machines.

- The see-saw is really a lever.

- How work input = work output.

- How to calculate work done by a lever.

With work input = work output as our starting point and armed with all those other equations, let's see how our first machine can help us out. For this machine, we have to do nothing more than visit our favorite playground.

We probably never realized how many machines surrounded us at the playground but we're here to focus on the "simple" see-saw. The see-saw or teeter-totter is much more than just a playground standard, it is also one of the most useful and plentiful of the simple machines.

A simple machine is by definition a device which can reapply and sometimes magnify your force to do work for you. It may, at the same time, change the direction of your F_e, which may be just what was needed to get the job done. Let's use our job to see how the see-saw or more correctly, the lever, does the work.

We'll start with the basic set up of a lever and observe how it can be altered as the need arises. We must begin with some rigid board or pole that is strong enough not to flex under the load we will use. Second, we need a fixed point for it to rotate on. A cross-beam of some kind, as in the see-saw, is crucial. We can fix the board to the cross-beam, if we choose but it must be free to rotate or swivel about this point. The point of rotation has a specific name. It is the <u>fulcrum</u>. It acts both to support the board, the load and your force and as a place for the board to rotate.

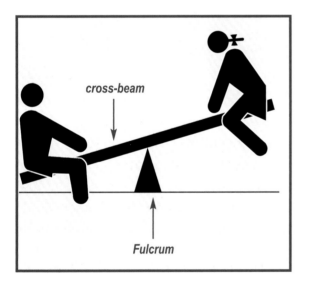

As with a standard see-saw, we'll place this fulcrum at the center of the board, so that it is "divided" into two equal arms. With one side down and the other side up in the air, we can set about to do our job. By placing our 1 kg. object on the "down" side, our lever is set for our part of the job.

According to the positioning of the fulcrum, we have set up a lever with arms of equal length. The side that has the 1 kg object will be where the work comes "out". The other side will be where we put work in. The "resistance" side looks exactly like the "effort" side, except it is down while the effort side is up.

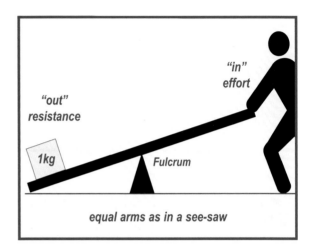

equal arms as in a see-saw

As we did before, we can compare distances or as in this case, lengths. The resistance arm length will equal the effort arm length. As before, we have a ratio, which describes the ideal mechanical advantage. We modify our original IMA equation as follows:

$$IMA = \frac{\text{Effort arm length}}{\text{Resistance arm length}}$$

For the present set-up, the IMA=1

Notice that we have yet to get involved with our F_e. So far, it looks like there is no particular advantage to this type of set-up. However, let's look at what happens when we actually apply a force.

As you may have done many times in the past, our job is to push downward on the

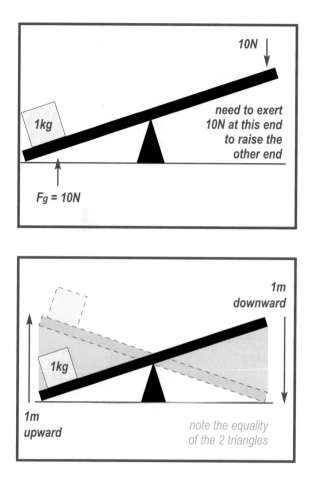

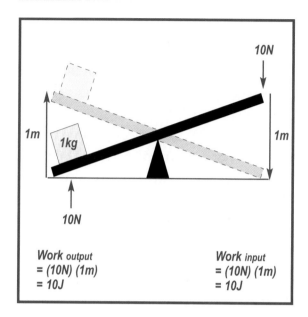

the job. Due to the geometry of the lever, we will have to apply our force over a 1m distance. Our work input will be

$$\text{work input} = (10N)\,(1m)$$
$$= 10J$$

effort side. As we apply our force, F_e, we feel the resistance of our 1 kg object on the other side. The force of I0N acting on the object due to gravity forces us to exert enough force to lift it off the ground. It needs I0N upwards, which according to our IMA should be in a ratio of 1:1. The geometry of this lever, being set up with equal arms, indicates that we will apply an equal force on the effort side. The one difference will be that we push <u>down</u> with I0N as the lever transfers this into a I0N <u>upward</u> force on the other side. A simple machine at work.

Our work, being put into the effort side, will be to apply a 10N downward force. We will have to keep pushing until our 1kg object is lifted the 1m we assigned to

Meanwhile, on the other side of our lever/see-saw, the 1 kg object will have been lifted 1m off the ground by the re-applied force. This force is also 10N as it is acting against the 10N force of gravity. The work done by the lever, our simple machine, will be

$$\text{work output} = (F_r)\,(d_r)$$
$$= (10N)\,(1m)$$
$$= 10J$$

This is the same as our work input. Since we are assuming a perfect world where no extra force is needed to overcome friction, the outcome is as expected.

$$\text{work input} = \text{work output}$$
$$10J = 10J$$

We can even show this result by checking our AMA.

$$AMA = \frac{F_r}{F_e}$$
$$= \frac{10N}{10N}$$
$$= 1$$

Just as with the arm length and the movement distances, all ratios are 1:1. The set up of this lever has allowed us to do the 10J job of <u>lifting</u> by doing 10J of work in a <u>downward</u> direction. The lever has helped us by changing the direction of our applied force, F_e.

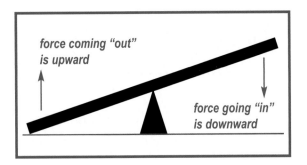

This redirection can be advantageous in many cases. It may be easier to push downward for example, by stepping on a lever to do a "job". If necessary, we can even sit on the end of the lever and use our body weight to work for us. But is this the only way a lever can help us?

Not at all. There are a number of ways that we can modify the arrangement of the lever. Let's start by repositioning the fulcrum. Say we put the fulcrum closer to the 1kg object. We can place the fulcrum so that the effort arm length is 4 times longer than the resistance arm length. Immediately, we can see that to raise the 1 kg object, the effort side will have to be pushed down much further than before. In fact, it will have to be pushed down 4 times further. This is the geometry of the lever.

According to our equation for IMA

$$IMA = \frac{\text{Effort arm length}}{\text{Resistance arm length}}$$
$$IMA = \frac{4}{1}$$
$$IMA = 4$$

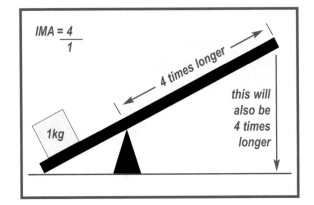

This ratio states that there is an ideal mechanical advantage of 4:1. Our effort distance will have to be 4 times greater than the resistance's distance. But what does that mean to us, the effort provider?

Here's how it works. The work we put in must <u>equal</u> the work we get out. That's how physics works. Work is the product of force and distance. As discussed, the distance will be 4 times larger. To keep the amount of work the same, we will in fact, have to apply a smaller force than before. It will be 4 times smaller than before. That is to say, it will be 1/4 the original force. It can be calculated as follows:

work input = work output

$$10J = (Fe) (de) \quad (de=1m)$$
$$(10J) = (\text{new } Fe) (\text{new } de)$$
$$\text{new } de = 4 \times 1m$$
$$= 4m$$
$$10J = (\text{new } Fe) (4m)$$
$$\frac{10J}{4m} = \frac{(\text{new } Fe) (\cancel{4m})}{\cancel{4m}}$$
$$\text{new } Fe = 2.5N$$

This time our simple machine, the lever, has not only redirected our force but has, maybe more importantly, multiplied our Fe by our mechanical advantage. We can now see why it is called mechanical advantage. The positioning of the fulcrum is the crucial factor in determining how "advantageous" our lever will be.

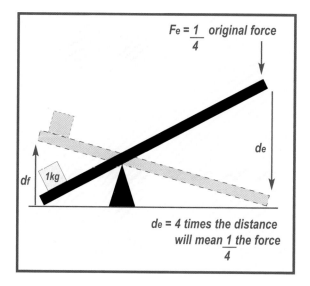

$Fe = \frac{1}{4}$ *original force*

de

df 1kg

de = 4 times the distance will mean $\frac{1}{4}$ *the force*

By moving the fulcrum closer to the 1 kg object we have created a set up where we apply a much smaller force. Let's check out what the AMA says.

$$AMA = \frac{Fr}{Fe}$$
$$= \frac{10N}{2.5N}$$
$$AMA = 4$$

There it is again. The AMA is saying that our force of 2.5N is being <u>multiplied</u> by a factor of 4 as it goes into performing our output work.

Let's try an example. A nail has been hammered partially into a board. We need to pull it out with a 200N force. There's no way you can do it by hand. The natural way to do the job is to use a crowbar. The claw is 4cm long whereas the handle is 40cm long. What force do you have to apply at the end of the crowbar to get the nail out?

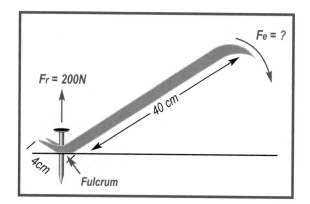

$Fr = 200N$

40 cm

4cm

Fulcrum

$Fe = ?$

To solve this problem, we first calculate the mechanical advantage of the crowbar. To do this, we use the arm lengths.

$$IMA = \frac{\text{effort arm length}}{\text{resistance arm length}}$$
$$= \frac{40cm}{4cm}$$
$$IMA = 10$$

We now know by what factor our Fe will be affected. To calculate the value, we'll use the AMA (which is equal to the same 10 as the IMA) and substitute in

$$AMA = \frac{Fr}{Fe}$$

$$10 = \frac{200N}{Fe}$$

$$Fe \times 10 = \frac{200N \times \cancel{Fe}}{\cancel{Fe}}$$

$$\frac{Fe \times \cancel{10}}{\cancel{10}} = \frac{200N}{10}$$

$$Fe = 20N$$

The answer is that we have to apply a force of only 20N to do the job a 200N force would do if it were applied directly on the nail. The lever has done its job of altering our input work into an output work. The extra distance we must push downward on the end of the crowbar is more than compensated for by the reduction in the Fe that is needed.

All single machines tend to follow this pattern. If we have to use a larger de then our reward is a smaller Fe.

A lever doesn't guarantee us an easier time to do the work. What do you think would happen if instead of moving the fulcrum towards the object, we moved it further away? A situation could arise where the resistance arm must be longer than the effort arm. For example, raising a railroad-crossing barricade. The set up usually has a very long arm across the road and a very short arm where the Fe is applied to raise the barricade when needed. The Fe will travel a short

distance, de, but to account for the greater Fe needed, there is a counter weight on the effort side to help apply the downward force.

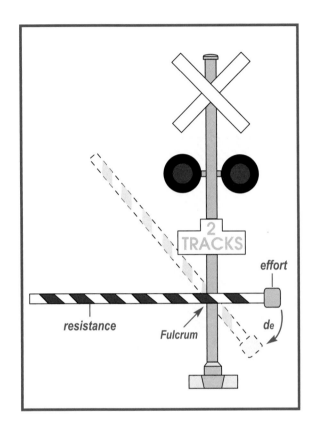

The next time you go to the playground, you will look at the see-saw with greater respect. This isn't the end of the story for our lever. We'll look at some of the other variations in everyday life in a later section. It's now time to look at the playground's second simple machine. Can you think what that might be?

Lesson # 5 – It's Uphill All the Way

Have you thought about it? What else could be a machine at the playground? The only other things that move are the swings and the merry-go-round. They are possible candidates but there is another playground standard that doesn't move yet is classified as a simple machine.

Recall that one job you studied was to raise a 1 kg object 1m off the ground. Again, if we look around the playground, there is another piece of equipment which would make this job easier, something that could help us with the lifting process. It's true that in the past, you've only used this to help you get down instead of up. Got it now? The slide.

A slide is a very simple device, which goes by other names like ramp, incline, grade, ladder, staircase, and slope. No matter what you call it, it always does the same thing. It bridges the gap between two elevations, usually in a straight line.

The idea of using a ramp or slope has been around for millennia. When tackling a mountain, there are those who must climb straight up whereas others may enjoy the less strenuous pace of walking up the gentle slopes leading up to the summit.

First, let's get rid of friction. We could use a system like an air hockey table and have the object float or put it on very good wheels. Whichever mechanism we use, let us say that the friction between the 1 kg. object and the surface has been reduced to zero. If we now give it a nudge, a push just large enough to overcome inertia, the 1 kg. object would start moving. With no friction present there would be no force to slow it down. It would, theoretically, move onward forever.

This object would be moving a distance but there would be no force doing the moving. By our calculation, that means no work is being done to move it horizontally.

$F = 0$ thus $(F)(d) = 0$. Remember, this is only true in a frictionless world.

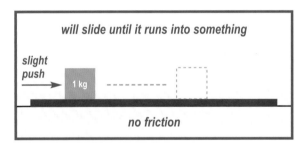

So, we have our 1 kg. object sliding across the length of our inclined plane which is not inclined yet. No work is being done to get it from one end to the other. You may have noticed something in the first step that sounds wrong. Wasn't there work done with that first small nudge we gave the object? Absolutely correct. That work went into giving the object its motion. At the end of the inclined plane we will have to apply a small force to stop it.

As you can tell, there will be a trade off. As with the lever, if the distance is longer, the force required will be less. That is the principle of the inclined plane as well. Let's see how that works out.

We begin with an inclined plane that is laying flat on the ground. It does sound weird but we have to start somewhere. With the 1 kg object on the board, if we push the object, it may in fact not move. It will have inertia, which is the "desire of an object to keep doing what it's doing". Since it is already stationary, it "wants" to stay put. The force of gravity that is also pulling down on it probably causing some friction between it and the floor. All are valid points to contend with.

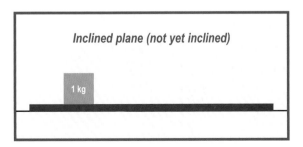

Otherwise, it will continue until it runs into something. The work we put in at the beginning is taken away at the end. The effect is that no work is being done as the object moves horizontally. With that understood, we go back to work.

Our job is to <u>lift</u> the 1 kg. object. Moving it horizontally doesn't enter into our job description. If we do have to move it horizontally, we will have to ignore any work done in that direction. Now, we can focus on lifting the object with the help of the inclined plane.

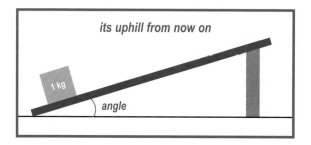

As soon as we raise our end of the inclined plane, it actually becomes inclined. Now, to move the object, we have to go "uphill". That slight nudge we used before won't do it. Something has happened. We now have to push it up the hill. But why?

Recall when we tried to lift the 1 kg object? Gravity was pulling downward against us. As soon as we tilted the inclined plane, we again were working against gravity. Although, this time, we have the help of the inclined plane. Using the idea of vectors, which involves angles, we can show how this comes about. It's a tough subject but let's see how we can simplify it.

As we begin to create an angle between the inclined plane and the horizontal surface it started on, this is what happens. Since gravity is always trying to pull the 1 kg. object straight downward, the inclined plane gets in the way of this downward force. As an angle is created, gravity's pull is "deflected" downhill. It is not as strong as when it pulls straight down though. The inclined plane acts to hold up the 1 kg. object but not all of it. We have to do part of the job.

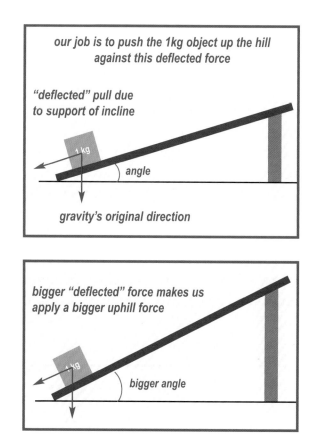

We have to use a force parallel to the inclined plane that is strong enough to do two things. The first is to stop it from sliding downward. We have to push uphill with enough force to overcome gravity's deflected force trying to slide it down the slope. We also have to add a little extra to help the inclined plane, which is partially holding it up.

These two amounts are controlled by the angle that the inclined plane is set at and trigonometry. The amount increases steadily as the angle increases but, since we've gotten rid of friction, the total will always be less than the force of gravity itself. In our job of moving the 1 kg. object 1m upward, the force will always be less than 10N. As with the lever, there will be a trade off.

To get an object 1m off the ground, we can set up several inclined planes. We could use one that is extremely gentle. It would have to be extremely long though. We could set up a ramp that is very steep, as in a ladder being propped up against a wall. This would be much shorter. By necessity and the law of right angled triangles, the inclined plane is always the hypotenuse of the triangle. This makes it the largest of the three sides. The height of the triangle represents how far up our object is lifted, our 1m.

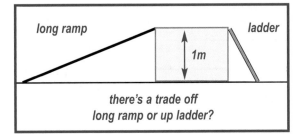

There's the trade off. In doing the job, we push along the inclined plane as it gets "raised" to the height of the triangle. The length of the inclined plane or ladder

lets us know whether we will be using a smaller or a larger force.

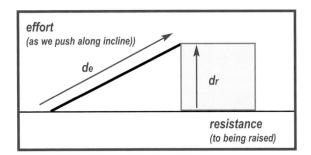

This sounds so much like the ideal mechanical advantage we saw in the lever. Exactly! As defined before,

$$IMA = \frac{\text{Effort arm length}}{\text{Resistance arm length}}$$

$$IMA = \frac{de}{dr}$$

In the case of the inclined plane, the "de" is the length of the incline. The "dr" represents the height to which we and the inclined plane together have "lifted" the 1 kg. object.

As mentioned before, any movement horizontally doesn't involve our "lifting" work. That means that the inclined plane does not have to go up in a straight line. We could wind the inclined plane around and make it into a spiral. It

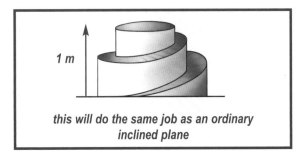

this will do the same job as an ordinary inclined plane

doesn't matter. The full length of the inclined plane and the final height off the ground are the only two factors. These two values control the value of the IMA. As before, this also determines the AMA of our simple machine, since IMA = AMA in our perfect frictionless scenario.

The AMA will still be the comparison of the F_r, which is still the force needed to "lift" our object upward, and our own F_e.

$$AMA = \frac{Fr}{Fe}$$

Back to our job that requires 10J of energy. If we set up a ramp that is 5m long that ends at a platform 1m high, we have an inclined plane ready to do some work. Using our IMA, we will determine how much F_e we need. Then, we can calculate the work input and compare it to the work output.

$$IMA = \frac{de}{dr}$$
$$= \frac{\text{length of inclined plane}}{\text{height of inclined plane}}$$
$$= \frac{5m}{1m}$$
$$IMA = 5$$

Since, no extra force due to friction is required

$$IMA = AMA$$
$$AMA = 5$$
$$AMA = \frac{Fr}{Fe} \quad (Fr = 10N \text{ as above})$$
$$5 = \frac{10N}{Fe}$$

$$Fe \times 5 = \frac{10N \times Fe}{Fe}$$
$$\frac{Fe \times 5}{5} = \frac{10N}{5}$$
$$Fe = 2N$$

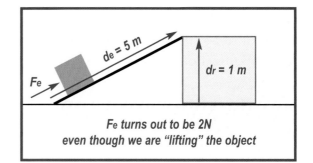

F_e turns out to be 2N even though we are "lifting" the object

By calculation, we only need to use 2N of applied force. That's a whole lot easier than lifting by hand directly upward with a full 10N. On the other hand, we must push the 1 kg. object all the way along the full length of the inclined plane. This is a full 5m long. The work we put in can be calculated as follows:

$$\text{work input} = (Fe)(de)$$
$$= (2N)(5m)$$
$$\text{work input} = 10J$$

This is the same as our original job. The same amount of work is being done. The advantage is that the inclined plane saved us some effort force by partially holding up the object as it was being moved. We did have to increase our distance but the trade-off is well worth it.

Say you had to move a refrigerator up a few stairs. It's true friction can't be totally overcome but it would seem that using some form of ramp will definitely ease the burden of having to lift the refrigerator straight up.

Let's go back to our 1 kg. object moving up the inclined plane. If we steepened the inclined plane, it would alter both the de and the Fe. For example, if you only had a 2m long board to use as a ramp to raise the object 1m, this is how it would affect our values

$$IMA = \frac{\text{length of inclined plane}}{\text{Height of inclined plane}}$$

$$= \frac{2m}{1m}$$

$$IMA = 2$$

Therefore $AMA = 2$

$$AMA = \frac{Fr}{Fe}$$

$$2 = \frac{10N}{Fe}$$

$$Fe \times 2 = \frac{10N \times Fe}{Fe}$$

$$\frac{Fe \times 2}{2} = \frac{10N}{2}$$

$$Fe = 5N$$

Our input force will now increase to 5N still less than the 10N maximum value of lifting.

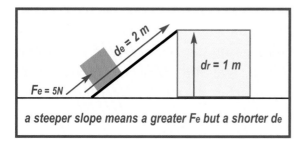

a steeper slope means a greater Fe but a shorter de

If you think that you've got the idea, let's try an example.

You're in your car, which has a total mass of 2000 kg and you want to go up a hill that has an elevation of 150m. There is a gentle sloping road that is 0.3 km long that will get you up to the top. Assuming no friction (we wish), what force does your engine have to exert to get the car up to the top? There are some big numbers here but it is exactly the same principle as our little job.

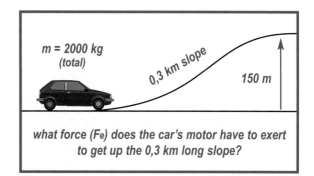

what force (Fe) does the car's motor have to exert to get up the 0,3 km long slope?

First, let's organize what we are given into input-output categories.

The total mass of car will give us the Fr (calculate the Fg of the car)

$$Fg = mg$$

$$= (2000 \text{ kg}) (10 m/s^2)$$

$$= 20000N$$

Thus, $Fr = 20000N$

The elevation of the hill is our "height" or dr.

Thus, $dr = 150m$

We can now calculate our work output or we can check out our IMA – AMA connection. To do that, we use the 0.3km long road as our de.

Thus, $d_e = 0.3$ km

But "km" don't match up with "m", so we have to convert by multiplying by 1000.

(1000m = 1k)
therefore $d_e = (0.3 \times 1000)$m
                    $d_e = 300$m

Now, we can calculate IMA and then our AMA (we've done this before so it shouldn't be too tough)

$$\text{IMA} = \frac{\text{length of inclined plane}}{\text{height of inclined plane}}$$

$$= \frac{300\text{m}}{150\text{m}}$$

$$\text{IMA} = 2$$

Thus, AMA = 2

which is $\text{AMA} = \dfrac{F_r}{F_e}$

$$2 = \frac{20000\text{N}}{F_e}$$

$$F_e \times 2 = \frac{20000\text{N} \times \cancel{F_e}}{\cancel{F_e}}$$

$$\frac{F_e \times \cancel{2}}{\cancel{2}} = \frac{20000\text{N}}{2}$$

$$F_e = 10000\text{N} \quad (\text{finally!})$$

The answer is that the engine has to deliver 10000N of force to drive the car up to the top of the hill.

The inclined plane is the second simple machine that came from the playground. As with the lever, we can see how the mechanical advantages can be calculated and how the work input is connected to the work output. There aren't too many variations we can do

with an inclined plane. We'll check some out later.

Next on the list though is a simple machine that does not come from the playground but you are familiar with it nonetheless.

Notes

_____
_____
_____
_____
_____
_____
_____
_____
_____
_____
_____
_____
_____
_____
_____
_____
_____
_____
_____
_____
_____
_____
_____
_____
_____

Lesson # 6 – And The Wheels Go Round and Round

Objectives:

- How to redirect your applied force.

- How work is done with a pulley.

- How pulleys can really increase your "strength".

- Finding the IMA the easy way.

The two machines we've seen so far have both come from the playground. This next machine is just about as common and has widespread applications. We do not know its origin, but it probably began when someone tried to lift an object, as we have done, by pulling it with a rope.

When you pull on the rope, it seems to pull back or at least resist your tug. As long as it is strong enough to withstand the force, you feel a tension in the rope. Just as with guitar strings you can feel the strength of this force in the tension of the string. In this way, our force of pulling on the rope is transmitted over to the object by way of the tension in the rope.

We begin by pulling one end of the rope. The force is transmitted by tension in the rope to the object where it pulls on the object. The rope is like the lever as it

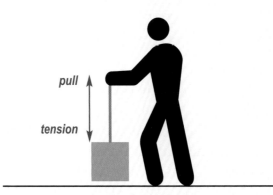

as you pull upwards, you feel the rope pull downwards

transmits our input force. Is that the machine? A simple rope?

When we find out that the pull upward isn't enough to move the object what can we do? Someone once had the idea of looping the rope over a strong overhead branch and then using its weight to help pull downward on the rope which would, through the transmission of tension pull upward on the object. Using body weight (the pull of earth's gravitational force) rather than pure muscular strength seems to be much easier and advantageous.

by putting the rope over the branch, you could use your body weight to help lift the object

This was the idea for our next machine. By throwing the rope over the branch, we are able to apply a force in one direction and yet have it do work in the opposite direction. Rescuing someone who has fallen into a pit by having the rope go over the edge is another variation. In all these situations, our applied force, F_e, is being redirected

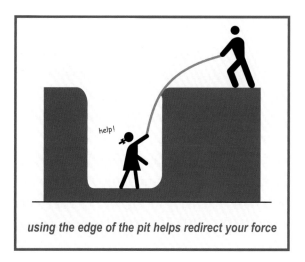

using the edge of the pit helps redirect your force

until it is applied to the object, where it meets the resisting force, F_r.

A serious problem in each example is that there will be a lot of friction. So much so, that the rope might break. We want to make certain that when we pull down, all our force is transmitted through the rope and "gets to the other side".

The pulley is a simple device. It is a wheel on an axle that can rotate freely with a groove or notch in the outer rim for a rope. Grooves were probably

created so that the rope would not move out of position. These grooves were also sanded down probably through use, as well as probably being oiled to reduce the friction. It would take the idea of using a wheel with a groove for the rope to begin the age of the pulley. There must be a way to fix the pulley so that we can pull "against" it without it moving. A pulley fixed to the ceiling, for example, is the same as the rope over the branch method. A pulley fixed in such a position has really only one function; to redirect our applied force, F_e.

Remember our job? If we attach a rope to our 1 kg object and run it through a fixed pulley, we will be ready to apply a force <u>downward</u> to lift it <u>upward</u>. Again, to lift upward, we'll need to use 10N. Since the rope transmits this force, we will pull downward with a force of 10N. Mathematically, that's not much of an advantage. In fact, the AMA is

$$AMA = \frac{F_r}{F_e}$$
$$= \frac{10N}{10N}$$
$$= 1$$

only equal to 1. Does this apply to the IMA as well?

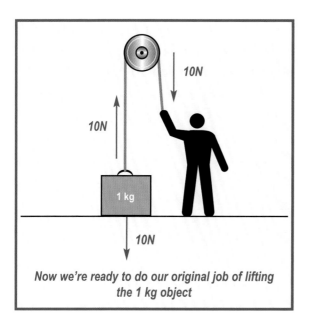

Now we're ready to do our original job of lifting the 1 kg object

Ropes and chains tend not to stretch very much when we pull on them. We will consider for our job, that there is no stretch at all. That would mean, to lift the object up by 1m, we have to pull 1m of rope towards us on the other side. That means that, $d_r = 1m$

as well as $d_e = 1m$. So, our IMA is

$$IMA = \frac{d_e}{d_r}$$
$$= \frac{1}{1}$$
$$= 1$$

Again, we have an advantage of only 1.

Nothing gained but we do get to pull <u>down</u> instead of lifting upward. This is an advantage and could save our backs.

If we check out the amount of work we put in, we'll find that we did the same 10J of work as we did before.

$$Work_{input} = (F_e)(d_e)$$
$$= (10N)(1m)$$
$$= 10J$$

In its first application, the pulley has redirected our force and therefore our work and nothing more. This is true for any situation or arrangement of <u>fixed</u> pulleys. Having a rope pass through a series of rollers/pulleys that are all fixed only changes directions. It may be advantageous to be standing in one place and have your force transmitted somewhere else. Pulleys must be used for more than just directional shifts. Let's see how.

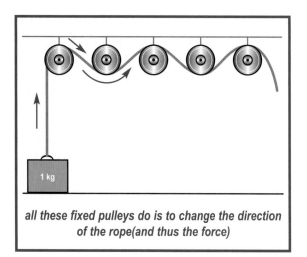

all these fixed pulleys do is to change the direction of the rope(and thus the force)

To show how pulleys can be used to a greater advantage, follow this discussion. If we try to lift our 1 kg object by ourselves, we must apply a force of 10N, correct? But if we get someone else to help in the lifting, the weight is shared between us. Now, we only need to apply 5N each. The more people involved in lifting, the less force we each need to supply.

If two ropes are attached to the 1kg object, each will be "lifting" with a 5N force.

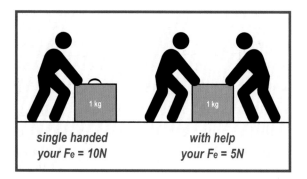

single handed
your Fe = 10N

with help
your Fe = 5N

Well, what if we attached a pulley to the object. By placing a rope through the

pulley, we can now hold both ends of the rope. Each side of the rope will have an upward force of 5N. (for simplicity, we won't count the extra weight of the pulley being lifted, OK?)

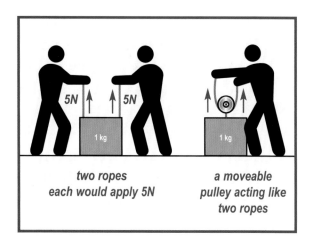

two ropes
each would apply 5N

a moveable
pulley acting like
two ropes

This means there is a tension of 5N passing through the rope from both sides. We're also standing there holding both ends of the rope. No advantage. Not yet!!

If we now attach one end of the rope to a hook, let's say, we can let go of that end and only have to hold up the other end. This time we will be lifting upward with a 5N force and not the previous 10N. Sounds advantageous to me.

If we check the AMA,

$$AMA = \frac{F_r}{F_e}$$
$$= \frac{10N}{5N}$$
$$= 2$$

We now have a set up with an advantage of 2. Due to the fact that there are "two ropes" holding up the pulley and the 1kg object, we seem to get an advantage of 2.

Now, we only have to lift with a 5N force. The moveable pulley "doubles" our force.

It's true that it is only one long rope and not two, but because the rope passes through the pulley, which is free to move, it acts like two ropes, each pulling up. This notion is critical, especially when we add a lot more pulleys to our system. A moveable pulley provides us with a mechanical advantage of 2.

Our input force has been reduced to only 5N down from the 10N we used before.

Does this mean that we get to do less work? Let's examine what happens when we try to lift the 1kg object with our 5N force. If we were to each hold the two ends of the rope, we would both have to raise the object 1m. Each rope would be raised 1m each. But with the moveable pulley, as you pull on one side, it shortens both sides. Using the pulley with one end of the rope fixed, 2m of rope would have to be pulled out to shorten both sides by 1m each. The 1kg object would be lifted 1m off the floor while we

will have pulled 2m of rope through the pulley.

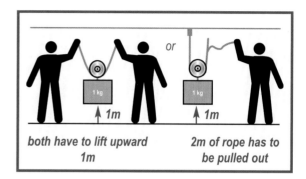

both have to lift upward 1m   *2m of rope has to be pulled out*

If we calculate the IMA using these values:

$$IMA = \frac{de}{dr}$$
$$= \frac{2m}{1m} \text{ (rope we pulled through)}$$
$$= 2$$

This is the same value as the AMA and the same as the number of ropes. It is for this reason that for pulley systems, we can use the short cut in determining the IMA. To do this we simply count the number of ropes that move up with the object by way of the pulley. It's that easy.

We can complicate the situation by adding a fixed pulley to the set up. Will this change our mechanical advantage? We stated before that a fixed pulley merely changes direction of the applied force. Why should that be different this time?

It might. It depends on where we tie the end of the rope. Say we attach the rope to the bottom of the fixed pulley, feed it through our movable pulley and then through the fixed pulley. As you can see, we are now in a position to pull downwards. If we check the object, we can see only two ropes holding it up. This suggests an IMA of 2.

In fact, it is 2. The fixed pulley does nothing more than anchors the rope and redirects our F_e. That's true, it is a large contribution but not to the IMA.

However, we could use the same two pulleys but change one thing, which would affect the IMA and subsequently our AMA. This time, let's tie the rope to the top of the movable pulley. Then send the rope over and through the fixed pulley. Now, thread the rope through the movable pulley and out the side. With this set up, we must pull upwards to get any movement.

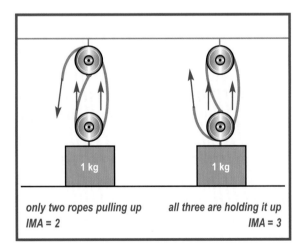

only two ropes pulling up
IMA = 2

all three are holding it up
IMA = 3

If we check carefully, we will find there are now three ropes "holding up" the 1kg object. (by way of the moveable pulley) As before, to lift the object 1m off the ground, each of these 3 rope sections has

to be shortened to do the job. In essence, we will pull 3m of rope to get the object to move only 1m.

$$IMA = \frac{de}{dr}$$
$$= \frac{3m}{1m}$$
$$IMA = 3$$

This pulley set up has a 3:1 ratio for mechanical advantage.

As we have seen, the job has not changed, thus the work we put in should not have changed (Remember, no extra work because we're excluding friction)

$$Work_{input} = Work_{output}$$
$$Work_{input} = (F_e)(de)$$

For this pulley system then, we can calculate our F_e

$$10J = (F_e)(3m)$$
$$\frac{10J}{3m} = \frac{(F_e)(3m)}{3m}$$
$$F_e = 3.33N$$

Our F_e has been reduced to only 3.33N. We should have seen this coming as there are three ropes holding up our 10N object.

Pulleys have a simplicity about them. As long as they turn freely, it makes life so much easier. Let's say we were helping out our roofer (from intro) who set up a pulley system to get the shingles up to the roof. If you pulled downward with a 200N force and this was able to lift 60kg (that's 600N of force) of shingles to the roof 3m up, how many ropes do you have to pull?

To solve this, we don't even need a diagram. We assume, as always, that there is no extra force needed due to friction, etc. That makes

$$IMA = AMA$$

Start with calculating the AMA.

$$AMA = \frac{Fr}{Fe}$$
$$= 600N \quad (Fr \text{ of the shingles})$$
$$= 200N \quad (\text{our applied force})$$
$$AMA = 3$$

That means that out IMA is also 3.

$$IMA = 3$$
And since $$IMA = \frac{de}{dr}$$

Our dr was stated as 3m. So,

$$3 = \frac{de}{3m}$$
$$3m \times 3 = \frac{de \times 3m}{3m}$$
$$de = 9m$$

We would have to pull out 9m of rope to do the job.

As we add more and more pulleys, we can keep changing our mechanical advantages. We'll look at some of these examples, as well as other types of machines and modifications in the last section of simple machines.

Notes

_____
_____
_____
_____
_____
_____
_____
_____
_____
_____
_____
_____
_____
_____
_____
_____
_____
_____
_____
_____
_____
_____
_____
_____
_____
_____

The Pulley

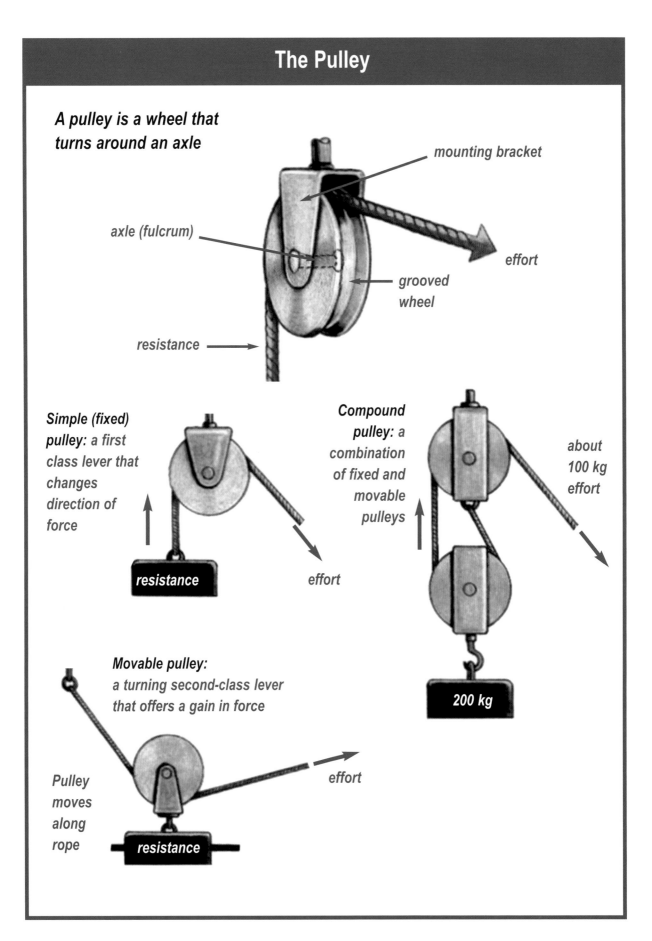

A pulley is a wheel that turns around an axle

mounting bracket

effort

axle (fulcrum)

grooved wheel

resistance

Simple (fixed) pulley: a first class lever that changes direction of force

resistance

effort

Compound pulley: a combination of fixed and movable pulleys

about 100 kg effort

200 kg

Movable pulley: a turning second-class lever that offers a gain in force

Pulley moves along rope

resistance

effort

Lesson # 7 – These Machines Are Simple, Too!

Objectives:

- Simple machines exist in many other forms.

- How an axe is related to an inclined plane.

- How a nutcracker is related to a wheelbarrow.

We've seen the three main types of simple machines. Others may have more and/or different classifications but whether you give them their own category, or group these machines together, they all use your input to create the machine's output. They also work simply.

We examined the lever, the inclined plane and the pulley as our three simplest machines. Well, the story doesn't end there. In this section, we'll look at several other variations of the above that can still be classed as simple machines and see that they are everywhere we look.

Following in no particular order, let's go back to the inclined plane to look for other applications of its principle. As you recall, the geometry of the triangle formed by the inclined ramp and the height is what creates its mechanical advantage. As you move the object along the slope, the inclined plane helps to support a lot of the object's weight. That

means it applies an upward force as you move along the surface.

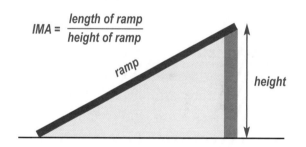

$$IMA = \frac{length\ of\ ramp}{height\ of\ ramp}$$

Imagine that we took a portable version of this, say, about 30cm long and tried to hammer it into a log. That's right, a wedge. Placed properly and struck correctly, it will split a log easily. It uses the principle of the inclined plane. An axe by itself is just a moveable form of a wedge.

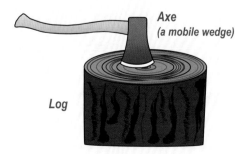

Axe
(a mobile wedge)

Log

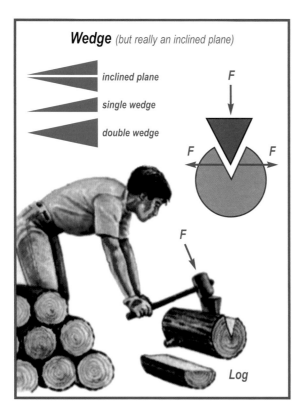

Wedge *(but really an inclined plane)*

inclined plane

single wedge

double wedge

F

F   F

F

Log

This principle can go a long way in explaining why nails are pointed and fence posts that are beveled at the end can be driven into the ground more easily. In carpentry, shims are used to position doors and windows. Without much effort, these large units can be moved by way of the shim, a simple wedge.

If we keep going on the inclined plane theme, we can come up with staircases and ladders. Each of these allows us to raise ourselves off the ground in a much easier way than climbing straight up. Both the stepladder and the staircase have the equivalent of the triangle set-up of the inclined plane. The advantage is in how high we rise as compared to the length of the incline. This is called the slope. As you can see, the inclined plane is a simple machine that is with you daily.

If you think that does it for the inclined plane, wait until you see how important the next variation is. First, look at the profile of an inclined plane. Now, imagine rolling it up around an upright cylinder. You can try it with a triangle cut out of paper and a pencil. When you're done, you will have a spiral. Imagine that this spiral was a ridge placed around a metal cylinder. What would you have? A screw.

Anything in the world that has a screw in it is being held together by a device

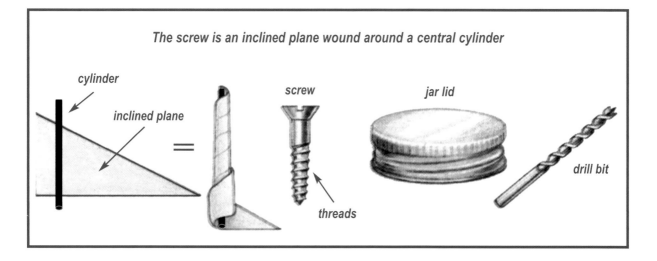

The screw is an inclined plane wound around a central cylinder

cylinder

inclined plane

=

screw

jar lid

threads

drill bit

based on the inclined plane. The gap from one edge to another as you go up the screw gives an indication of its mechanical advantage. A smaller pitch means more turns of the screwdriver but less force is needed. This makes the screw one of the most important applications of a simple machine. It can be used in delicate situations as in watch mechanisms or to pull and hold together large beams in the construction industry. With the addition of a lever arm, a screw jack can lift a house.

Perhaps you've seen or used a posthole digger. This is also a good example of how a screw as a spiral inclined plane can do a job. The gap between the grooves is large enough so that the apparatus is "screwed" into the earth, the loose earth moves up the "screw" and out of the hole. This is a modern day version of what Archimedes did when he invented the device to lift water from the river. Simple machines have been around a long time, haven't they?

post hole digger

archimedes screw used to remove water from river to irrigate land

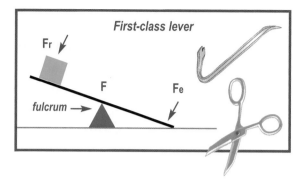

First-class lever

Fr

F

Fe

fulcrum →

Aside from the inclined plane leading to various other simple machines, the lever also has its many variations. To begin with, the lever we used before is considered a first-class lever. This is because the fulcrum is between the input and the output. In that form, the crowbar and even a pair of scissors apply the rules of simple machines. Would you have thought that using a broom is the same as a see-saw?

If we change the position of the fulcrum, two other arrangements can be made. By placing the fulcrum at an end and having the resistance between it and the applied force, we set up a second-class lever. Again, the arm lengths, as measured from the fulcrum, determine the IMA. By the relative positions, we can see how a wheelbarrow is a second-class lever. The longer the handle the

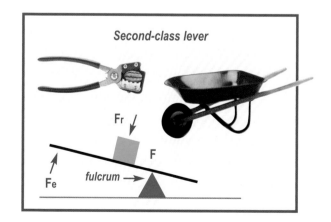

Second-class lever

Fr

F

Fe

fulcrum →

easier it is to move heavy loads. A nutcracker is a smaller version that takes your Fe and multiplies it to obtain enough force to crack the nut.

A third arrangement places the fulcrum, or point of rotation, next to the applied force. The resisting force is out further than the effort force. In this third-class lever, the IMA is less than 1. We don't get an advantage with our forces but how else could you fish? The fulcrum is where you hold onto the rod at the base. Your other hand, the Fe, grabs the rod higher up. This leaves the fish as the resistance at the top of the rod. Third-class lever all the way.

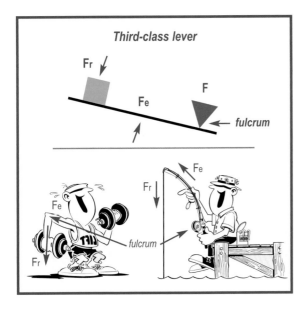

Third-class lever

Speaking of your hand, it is attached to your arm. The way it moves is controlled by a third-class lever arrangement. Your elbow acts as the fulcrum. Your muscles are attached up the arm with the load being placed in your hand. The swinging of a hammer is another example of a third-class lever in motion. In summary, third-class levers require an effort

greater than the resistance. However, they are useful because they enable us to increase the distance moved by the resistance in a short period of time. Also, some levers of this type enable us to grasp objects conveniently.

We're not finished with levers yet. Another variation involves some special maneuvers. To begin with, we set up a first-class lever that has an equal arm length. More than likely, we'll choose the longer arm to get the best advantage. Then we make certain that this lever can rotate in a full circle. By doing this, the two ends of the lever have described two circles. One large one with a smaller one "attached" to it. As we rotate the outer circle, it moves the inner circle. The ratio of the arm lengths matches that of the ratio of the radii. This gives us the opportunity to apply a small force to rotate the outer circle; the wheel will translate into a greater force which comes from the smaller circle, the axle.

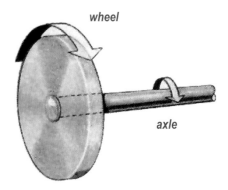

wheel

axle

A set up like this reminds me of a doorknob. The larger diameter knob is attached to a smaller diameter shaft. A small force exerted to rotate the knob translates into a larger force turning the latch mechanism. This technique is similar to using pliers, (a first-class lever) to turn a bolt (an inclined plane).

If we stay with the "double circle" set up what we actually have is called a wheel and axle. The outer "circle" is represented by the wheel with the smaller "circle" representing an axle. Many examples of this machine come to mind. Your car's steering wheel is a great example. Even in older times, when a well was dug, they more than likely used a wheel and axle mechanism to haul up the water bucket. The basic handle type pencil sharpener that was used to sharpen the pencil, which was used to write this chapter is based on the wheel and axle.

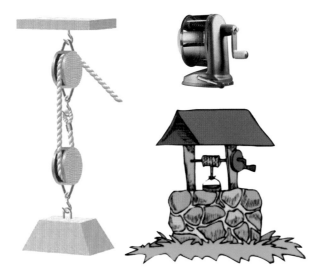

The last of our simple machines to be modified is the pulley. The pulley itself is not changed, only the number and arrangement is varied. As more pulleys are added to the system, the mechanical advantage can increase significantly. Sailing ships still use much of the same system developed long ago. By housing several pulleys together in a "block", a system called "block and tackle" can be created. This system can multiply the effort of a team of men as they pull on the rope to lift the massive sails. By using a chain instead of a rope, you can guard against the rope breaking. This is especially important when hoisting an engine out of a car.

As you can see, simple machines and their "offspring" are used everywhere and for all types of functions. You should now be able to reread this unit's opening section and identify the many different simple machines at work.

Notes

_____
_____
_____
_____
_____
_____
_____
_____
_____
_____
_____
_____
_____
_____
_____
_____
_____
_____
_____
_____
_____

Unit 2 – Questions

After all that work you've just done you should be able to answer these questions.

1. What are the three different ways for designating direction that we discussed?

_____

_____

_____

2. What is the weight of a 250g baseball?

_____

3. If an applied force of 25N moves an object horizontally over a distance of 3m, how much work was done against friction?

_____

4. How much work is done to lift a 3kg box onto a shelf 1.2m above the floor?

_____

5. If a lever is set to have an IMA of 3/1 and apply a 5N force, what force does the lever exact as output?

_____

6. What force is required to push a 2kg object up a 6m long ramp that is 1.5m high?

_____

7. What is the IMA of this pulley system?

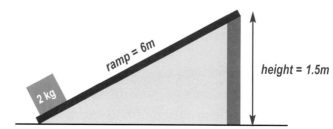

8. If the IMA of a pulley system is 5, then what F$_e$ do if we need to lift a 200N object?

_____

9. Name a variation of a

• Inclined plane _____

• Lever _____

• Pulley _____

SIMPLE MOTION

Simple Motion

Lesson #1 – Is It Moving?

Objectives:

• How we check for movement.

• Movements that you may not be able to see.

• The two parts that define motion.

Introduction

It's a hot, summer's day. You've finished all that yard work. The lawn chair is truly comfortable and the iced tea tastes great. With your eyes closed, you can hear your neighbor's lawn mower. Some kids are playing down the street, when their ball gets away and bounces off your head.

After listening to their sincere apologies, you toss the ball back. Sitting back down to enjoy the sun, you notice some dark clouds on the horizon. Will those storm clouds come your way? You stare at the clouds and try to see if the clouds are actually moving.

After a minute of staring aimlessly, you can't tell which way they are moving. Or if they are moving at all. Is that possible?

No movement at all? As you ponder this thought, your house's shadow starts to inch its way across the spot where you're sitting. You pick up your chair and shift it to a new spot.

All comfortable again, you spy a snail making its way across the lawn. Is it moving or isn't it? It's really hard to tell. You stare intently, waiting, watching, and trying to see its movement. Out of the corner of your eye you notice some leaves rustling. You turn your head but you're not sure if you saw a squirrel scamper up the tree. It moved so fast, it was hard to catch.

Anyway, you decide it doesn't matter. You're not going to move for anything. You're just going to sit there and not move at all. As you relax, you feel the ground tremble. What's going on?

Oh, it's just a truck passing through your street. Not an earthquake.

Well, your desire to not move is finally fulfilled. You may not be moving, but there does seem to be a lot of motion going on all around you. It's almost impossible to get away from movement. It's everywhere. Sometimes, it's obvious; sometimes it's really hard to tell. But all types of motion share some common elements and since this is a scientific discussion of motion, be prepared to study how we describe and measure it.

After that day in the sun, we've got to get down to business. We've got to get moving. In fact this whole chapter is about movement. Detecting it, measuring it, defining it. To study it properly, we're going to need a pencil, a calculator, a ruler and some graph paper. Keeping track of motion will take all these things.

To start, we'd better get some idea of what motion is. We could start with something that is not moving and work from there. So, any ideas for something that isn't moving? I guess it would be anything that's not going anywhere.

The key must be that it's not changing its position. The object is staying in the same place. Mountains tend to do that. Stay in the same place, that is. But how did they get there in the first place? Didn't the islands of Hawaii move out of the bottom of the ocean? Weren't the continents once all stuck together as one? All these events did occur but they took forever (or at least, a really long time).

With our ability to observe movement, even if we watch a mountain for a whole day, I don't think we'll get to see it move. We would have to use something more sensitive than our eyesight to detect that type of movement. Geologists have been using lasers to detect even the smallest shift in the earth. It's really important in areas of California for example because they're trying to predict when the earth's crust will move enough so that we can see it.

For our purposes though, we can agree that mountains, etc. are not moving? We need someplace solid to start from. If we can't rely on the ground beneath our feet to not move, what can we use? Wait, are you going to argue the point about the ground (that is, the earth), is also moving?

The earth, as a planet in our solar system, is in fact moving. We know this because we have day and night which means the earth rotates and we have summer and winter where the angle of the sun is different. The earth must be moving. Yet, we don't feel it. I guess that's because it's so big it's hard to measure its movement.

To get back to defining movement, I guess we're beginning to see that movement involves changing position. That is, not staying in the same place. A second factor that must occur simultaneously is that it takes time to change positions. For our mountains and continents, the change in position is really small and the time frame is extremely long. With these two factors together, it's impossible for us to measure these with a ruler and a watch.

That is really the basic principle of this chapter. To describe motion, we must be able to measure it. There are lots of other motions that we can't measure. Let's get those out of the way before we take out the yardstick and the stopwatch. Aside from the earth, we've been taught since we were young about the universe and the big bang. Whatever started the process, it is definitely continuing but only astronomers can prove it, with telescopes like the Hubble. That is motion on the galactic scale.

At the completely opposite extreme, everything is made up of atoms. These atoms are composed of even smaller particles. The most interesting particle is the electron. As small as an atom is, the electron is even smaller, yet it moves. It moves so fast that we can't really measure its movement. As soon as we can get a bead on it, it's gone somewhere else. The best we can do is approximate where it's moving. These are called orbitals. Special devices are needed to get even close to observing this special motion.

Those are the extremes. We're somewhere in between. At the human scale, we can observe motion in a variety of ways. Playing golf, you may toss a few blades of grass to see which way the wind is blowing. The sound of screeching tires tells you someone is trying to move way too quickly. When you catch a foul ball at the baseball game, you certainly can tell that the ball is moving. You didn't realize that your nose also detects motion. How often have you sniffed the air to determine where that smell is coming from?

The normal way that we observe motion though is by sight. When we look at an object, we perceive its position. As we continue to watch, our brain compares the images and if there has been a change in position, we can detect it. If the background for the object alters (like in those really old movies), we "see" the object move. We can be fooled somewhat but some type of movement will have taken place.

Regardless of how we perceive it, movement always has a change in position and it requires time to take place. From here on in, we're going to define the fundamental units of measuring this movement and how we can put these measurements together into very special formulas that describe the motion. So get your calculator ready for the next section.

Lesson # 2 - Just an Average Motion

Since we've just indicated that for movement to occur an object must change positions and that this change takes time, we can get down to the measuring of these events. Let's start with simply a ball rolling on the ground. As it rolls across your lawn, you may be thinking about the kids who threw it or the fact that it is changing position during the time you've watched it. Both of these can be measured.

This measurement will be a measure of the distance traveled by the ball. It answers the question of "how far?" Throughout this entire chapter, we'll limit ourselves to this concept of "how far?" without confusing the issue too much with directions. You first want to get the normal interpretation down pat before we complicate it with the issue of <u>going there</u> and <u>coming back</u>.

How far is it going?
How long will it take?

The change in position is really another way of describing how far it has moved. A yardstick or tape measure could be easily used to get the value for this movement. In physics, we usually measure "how far?" in meters (about 3 ft.)

How far is it going?

How long will it take?

Meanwhile, it has definitely taken time for the ball to travel its distance. By using a stopwatch, we can time the "how long?" it took to go along with the "how far?" we measured with the tape. The "how long?" is usually measured in seconds. It's true that snails, for example, do take minutes if not longer to get anywhere but to be able to make comparisons between different object's motions, it's best to pick a standard unit. For our discussion, let's use meters for short distances and kilometers (1000 meters) for long ones. Correspondingly, let's use seconds for quick events and hours for longer trips. Armed with these parameters, we can begin to investigate the connection between "how far?" and "how long?"

In Physics, we also use abbreviations or symbols to represent specific measurements. In this case, we're going to use "d" to represent our distance and, you guessed it, "t" to represent our time. If we go back to the ball rolling across the lawn, we can now properly label the event. It may have rolled 12 meters and taken 3 seconds to get there. With these two values, we are ready to define an important concept in Physics. The concept is "how fast?" You would normally refer to this as speed. By combining the "how far?" with the "how long?", we can define the answer to "how fast?"

That is to say,

$$\text{how fast?} = \frac{\text{how far?}}{\text{how long?}}$$

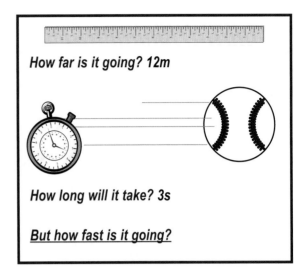

How far is it going? 12m

How long will it take? 3s

But how fast is it going?

In Physics, we say

$$\text{speed} = \frac{distance}{time}$$

For speed, one would think we could use the letter "S". Since we have to mesh these formulae with the ones you'd find in Physics textbooks, we'll use the standard letter "v".

This "v" stands for a more specific type of speed called velocity. The difference between speed and velocity has to do with taking into account direction. For our discussion we can use the symbol, "v" without having to report about East and West, etc.

The equation looks like this then,

$$v = \frac{d}{t}$$

Since the units for the distance are measured in meters and those for the time are measured in seconds, we get a combined unit for the speed, v. The unit is the fraction, meters/second abbreviated as, m/s. This is read as "meters per second." It describes how fast our object moves by describing the number of meters traveled in a second. With our data,

$$d = 12m$$
$$t = 3s$$

we have, by substituting into our equation.

$$v = \frac{d}{t}$$
$$v = \text{(hit those calculator buttons and get...)}$$
$$v = 4m/s$$

Stated properly, the ball had a speed of 4m/s.

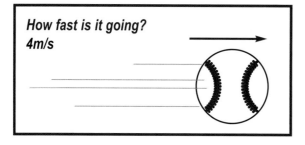

To be accurate though, we don't know how fast it actually moved during every second of its movement. All we can say is that over the 4 seconds we measured, it seemed to travel 4 meters each second. In other words, it <u>averaged</u> 4m/s. We should include this in our equation. We can modify it like this,

$$v_{avg} = \frac{d}{t}$$

We can now properly say that the ball had an average speed of 4m/s as it rolled across the lawn.

 A pitched baseball takes about 0.6 seconds to get from the pitcher to the catcher, 18 meters (approx.) away. What is the speed of the ball? We start by setting up the information in a list. It seems too simple to do this now, but later we'll have lots of data to contend with. Get used to organizing it.

So,

$$d = 18m$$
$$t = 0.6s$$
$$v_{avg} = ?$$

$$v_{avg} = \frac{d}{t}$$
$$= \frac{18m}{0.6s}$$
$$= 30m/s$$

That gets us the average speed but it's also possible to know the average speed and the time, and figure out the distance covered during that time. We can either rewrite the equation or substitute into the original equation and perform some algebra. Let's try both methods to see which you prefer.

The rearranged equation would take the form of

$$V_{avg} \quad \frac{d}{t}$$

$$t \times V_{avg} = \frac{d \times \cancel{t}}{\cancel{t}} \quad \text{(multiply both sides by t)}$$

$$t \times V_{avg} = d \quad \text{(which can be written for d =)}$$

$$d = V_{avg} \times t$$

(how far = how fast x how long)

We now have a modified form of the equation.

Let's try a problem. How far will you travel if you average 70 km/hr (kilometers per hour) for 3 hours.

Method 1 – the rearranged equation

$$d = V_{avg} \times t$$
$$= 70 \text{ km/}\cancel{hr} \times 3 \text{ }\cancel{hr}$$

(note how the "hr" cancelled out)

$$d = 210 \text{ km}$$

Method 2 – Substitute into the original equation

$$V_{avg} = \frac{d}{t}$$

$$70 \text{ km/hr} = \frac{d}{3 \text{ hr}} \quad \text{(multiply both sides by 3 hr to "move" it)}$$

$$3 \text{ hr} \times 70 \text{ km/hr} = \frac{d \times 3\cancel{hr}}{3\cancel{hr}}$$

$$210 \text{ km} = d$$

The same result. Great! So, what's the difference you may ask? In method 1, we used a different form of the equation. This would mean having a different equation for each unknown we want to find.

In our present formula, we only have 3 variables. Later, we will have more complex equations. Many feel it is safer to substitute the values into the equation and then let algebra take over. If you wish to reorganize an equation, go for it, but you are on your own.

The past two examples seemed easy enough. Good job, but this next one will be harder. This "motion" will be done in stages.

You're driving from home to see a friend who lives 600 km away. You drive for 2-1/2 hrs before you take a 15-minute stop to get gas. You drive another 1-1/2 hrs before you take a 45-minute "rest" stop. You finish the last part of the trip in only 1 hr. You proudly knock on your friend's door ready to tell him how fast you did the trip. When you give him the facts and your version of your average speed he says you've made an error and explains the right way to do the calculation.

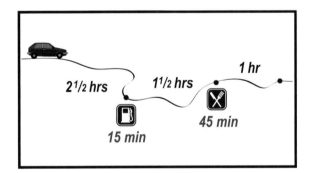

What actually was the average speed?

Okay, here's the proper way to get the answer.

We both agree that the distance driven is 600 km, we probably will disagree though on the time factor.

Recall

$$\text{how fast?} = \frac{\text{how far?}}{\text{how long?}}$$

The "how long?" refers to how long it took to <u>complete</u> the whole trip. This means "rest" stops must be included into the time, the <u>total</u> time.

In this question, the time is...
$$= 2\text{-}1/2 \text{ hrs} + 15 \text{ min} + 1\text{-}1/2 \text{ hrs} + 45 \text{ min} + 1 \text{ hr}$$

Adding hours and minutes together can be tricky.

Add the minutes first,
$$15 \text{ min} + 45 \text{ min} = 60 \text{ min}$$
Luckily, this is 1 hr.

Now, add the fractions of an hour,
$$1/2 \text{ hr} + 1/2 \text{ hr} = 1 \text{ hr}$$
Also, 1 hr.

So, all together, the total time is
$$t = (2+1+1) + (1) + (1)$$
$$= 6 \text{ hrs.}$$

We can now finish off the question.

$$V_{avg} = \frac{d}{t}$$
$$= \frac{600 \text{ km}}{6 \text{ hrs}}$$
$$= 100 \text{ km/h}$$

The average speed for the whole trip is 100 km/h

$$V_{avg} = \frac{\text{how far (total distance)}}{\text{how long (total time)}}$$

Try this last question to see if you've got it.

A bus driver runs a round trip route between 3 cities. It takes 5 hrs for the 400 km trip to the first city. Reloading the bus takes 30 minutes. On the road again, it takes 3 hrs 15 min to get to the second city, which is 220 km away. After a 1 1/4 hr supper, he drives back to his home city which is 280 km away in 4 hrs. What average speed did he have for the day's drive?

Do the question by yourself first before you look at the answer.

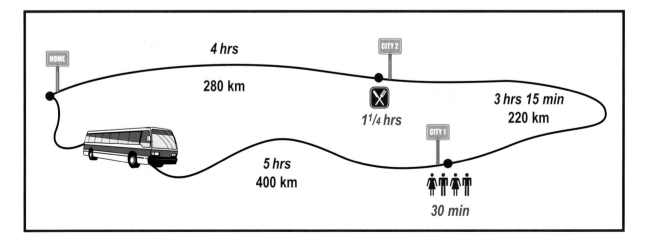

Answer:

d (how far) = 400 km + 220 km + 280 km
$\qquad$ = 900 km

t (how long) = 5 hrs + 30 min +
$\qquad$ 3 hrs 15 min + 1-1/4 +
$\qquad$ 4 hrs
$\qquad$ = 14 hrs

$$V_{avg} = \frac{900 \text{ km}}{14 \text{ h}}$$
$\qquad$ = 64.3 km/h (approx)

This section has shown the application of the most fundamental equation for motion.

$$V_{avg} = \frac{d}{t}$$

In later sections, we will add to it and adjust it to fit our needs. Sharpen your pencil and get your graph paper ready because we'll need it where we're going next.

Notes

_____
_____
_____
_____
_____
_____
_____
_____
_____
_____
_____
_____
_____
_____
_____
_____
_____
_____
_____
_____
_____
_____
_____
_____

Lesson # 3 - Steady as She Goes

So far we have one equation to describe motion. As we have seen, it incorporates long distances, rest stops and the like. It averages it all out in the equation:

$$V_{avg} = \frac{d}{t}$$

In this section, we're going to examine a different application of this same equation. This time, we're not looking for averages though.

Imagine you're on the highway on a nice long stretch of road. Traffic is light and the scenery is pleasant but not exciting. Isn't it great to be able to turn on the cruise control and sit back? The idea behind "cruise" is that it keeps the car moving at a fixed speed, always the same number of kilometers per hour. If we ignore the slight adjustments due to the ups and downs of the road, we'll just say that you're traveling at a fixed or constant speed.

So there you are, driving along at a speed of 100 km/hr, respecting the speed limit. Your speedometer registers the same value all the time. Pretty monotonous, but in Physics, this type of motion is important. Moving at a constant speed is referred to as <u>uniform motion</u>. It's the consistency and steady pace that makes it "uniform."

In driving down the highway, you cover a distance in a length of time. There's a "how far?" and "how long?" which must lead to a "how fast?" Well, we use the same equation as we did before.

That's right,

$$V_{avg} = \frac{d}{t}$$

"cruise control"

But this time our v_{avg} never changes. It always stays the same. The symbol, v_{avg}, has taken on a second meaning, that of our constant speed. When an object is in uniform motion, we find its constant speed by distance over time as before. This time, it is much more confirmed. We must <u>start</u> at a point and travel onward with no stops. The motion must be continuous <u>and</u> be uniform.

For motion to be uniform, it must be constant, steady, fixed. Get the picture? In fact, a picture, actually a math picture known as a graph, is really the best way to show this concept. But first, let's get out of the car and take a walk. A walk at a constant speed.

So, here we are walking at a nice steady pace. What do you notice? There is a rhythm to our steps. We seem to be taking the same number of steps per interval of time. Let's say, we take 2 steps every second. If each step is 1 meter long (just to make the math easier), we walk a (2x1m) distance every second. If we walked for 20m, it would take us,

    2m   in   1 sec.
    20m   in   ? sec.
                    ...10 seconds.

And if we walked for 25 seconds, we would travel a distance of,

    1 sec   2 m.
    25 sec   ? m.
                    ...50 m.

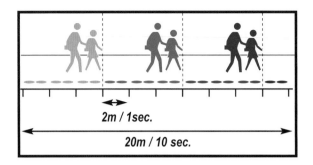

This concept revolves around the equation.

$$v_{avg} = \frac{d}{t}$$

In this example, we walk 2m each second

or $v_{avg} = 2m/s$

we also walked 50m in 25 sec., which is the same as 2m/s. Hence, the concept of uniform motion connects the distance to the time. For convenience sake, we can rewrite the equation to express this as

$$d = v_{avg} \times t$$

So, we have our equation set up and we're walking at our steady pace.

As we pass a landmark, we begin to record how far we travel and the time it takes us. It can be set up in a chart to collect our "data." When we begin our count, we have to start at t = 0 and d = 0. We then measure "how far" we travel against "how long" it takes us.

If we move as stated, at 2m/s we will find that after 3 seconds, we will have moved 6 meters. Here is an example of a data table showing our movement.

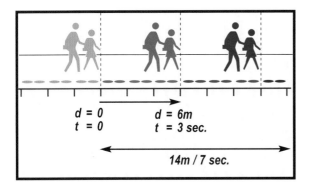

d = 0
t = 0

d = 6m
t = 3 sec.

14m / 7 sec.

time (sec)	distance (m)
0	0
3	6
5	10
12	24
20	40
30	60

At this point, it can get too boring to keep count. You can see the pattern even though the measurements weren't recorded in a specific pattern. Somehow, within this table is the fact that we were moving at 2m/s.

The way to show this pattern is to draw a picture of it. Not an actual picture but a mathematical one. This is called a graph. Since both time and distance begin at 0, we'll start both scales at this point. We then extend the scales horizontally to the left for time and vertically upward for distance.

Each of these lines will be a "ruler" for us to locate our data points.

You're right; this is just like the X and Y-axis from math class, only this time we're only setting up one quadrant.

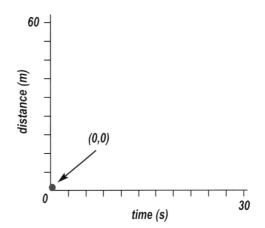

To set up the graph properly (as we'll need to do more of these later), we check to see what our last and largest value of "time" is. We then decide how to divide up the time line" to fit from 0 to our maximum value. Remember, it is a type of ruler and must be marked off evenly. The same is done for the distance scale, which is on the Y-axis.

Once the two axes are set, we locate our individual points. Our first point of (0,0), that's time first, followed by distance, is easy enough to find. At the origin, (the corner of the graph) we place a dot to mark its location. Our next data point is 3 seconds and 6 meters. We go to 3 on the time scale and then go up as high as 6 meters on the distance scale. We put our second dot on the graph.

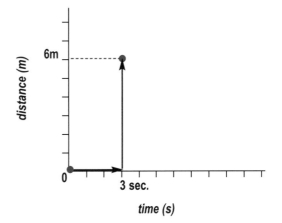

By locating each of the other data points, we will have "drawn a picture" of our motion. Stand back and check your artistry. Wait, doesn't it look like you could draw a perfect straight line from the (0,0) all the way to the (30,60) point. Why don't you do it? It would complete the picture.

With the line in, the graph is now complete. The record of our walking at a steady pace of 2m/s is now pictured clearly. You don't see it? Well, isn't the graph "moving"? It starts at the bottom left and "moves" upwards towards the right. As a matter of fact, if we check how quickly the graph "moves", that is how quickly it rises as compared to how quickly it moves horizontally (runs), we might then have our 2m/s speed.

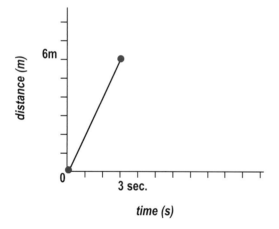

To check out this rise and run stuff, let's get the rules straight.

First, what we are about to do is calculate the slope of the graph. That word truly describes what the graph is doing, doesn't it? It does have a slope, an angle. In fact, it has only one unchanging slope. Didn't we have one

unchanging speed? It seems that the graph's slope may in fact be our constant speed.

Second, to get the slope we must follow a very strict protocol. We must

1. pick two places on the line, (choose the ones that are easy to locate)

2. from pt.1 to pt.2, we have to get the distance travelled (check the "rise" from pt.1 to pt.2)

3. for the same 2 points, we need to know how long it took (check the "run" along the time scale from pt.1 to pt.2)

4. finally, we use this equation

$$\text{slope} = \frac{rise}{run}$$

this will give us a distance value over a time value.

When this is done, we get a slope of 2m/s (keep the units with the data). You can check it out for yourself, but no matter which 2 points you pick, the answer will always turn out to be 2 m/s.

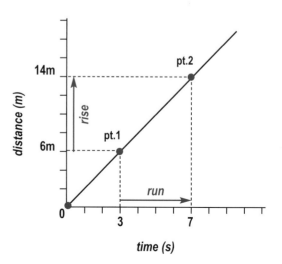

From this little example, two main ideas should come across. One of them is that if you move with a constant speed, your distance-time graph is going to be a straight line. Secondly, the slope of this line will give you the speed at which you were moving. That's pretty impressive for a straight line, to be able to give us that much information.

If the graph is so good at telling us how fast we're going, how would it "tell us" that we're not going anywhere? For example, if we walked along and then decided to stop for a few seconds, say to tie a shoelace, then continue on. I wonder how the graph would show that? For a few seconds, our distance wouldn't change and then it would continue from that point onwards. Try to sketch the graph without looking at my version.

Were you able to get the graph to show our "stop" by a flat line? This flat line section does tell its own special story. First, since it's straight, something is staying constant. It turns out to be our position. We are "constantly" not moving.

Second, the flat line does have a value for its slope. You probably want to argue that the line isn't rising. You're right. No rise! This means the slope has a value of 0. Our speed is 0. It's all true since we did stop moving.

To test you out on this new information, plot a graph of the following data. Then, identify how many stops were made and how fast the movement was between stoppages. Here goes.

time (s)	distance (m)
0	0
3	3
5	9
7	21
9	21
12	21
15	27
20	31

If you've done it properly, you should get the same answers as this. (see diagram)

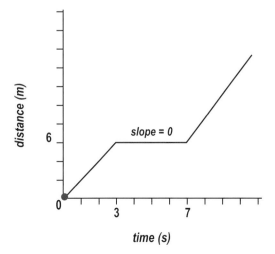

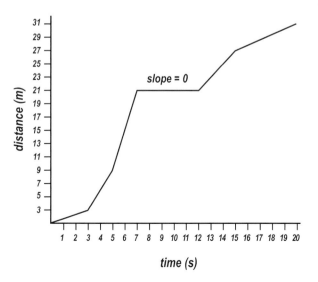

A review of constant motion will show how the equation $v = \dfrac{d}{t}$ and doing the slope of the d-t graph arrive at the same answer. Both tell us how fast we're moving, albeit at a constant rate. We'll deal with other rates later. For now, one last graph to draw.

We agree that we're moving at a steady, constant speed. If we were to collect data for time versus speed, it would be pretty boring. For each time interval, we have the same speed. If we were to plot a graph of speed versus time, it would show our constant speed but in a different way.

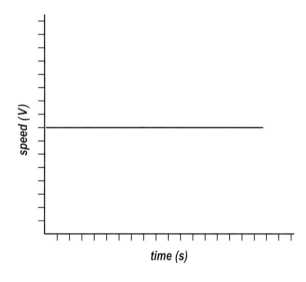

This time the graph goes straight across at a constant level, a different way to show the same story. We'll go into the story of speed-time graphs later.

For now, we know how constant speed can be expressed mathematically as well as graphically. In the next section, we tackle not-so-constant speed.

Lesson # 4 - Let's Speed Things Up

Objectives:

- The effect of speeding up on the distance-time graph.

- Its effect on a speed-time graph.

- The definition of acceleration.

- A new equation for motion.

Moving at a constant speed may have been great for a walk in the park or cruising down the highway or flying in a plane but the world doesn't move at a constant speed all the time. Everyday life does not involve objects that are always in motion at constant speed. Speeds change.

For now, let's just consider the process of speeding up. How are the distances and time data going to be affected when we speed up? Can we still use our equation of $v = \dfrac{d}{t}$?

Let's go through this one step at a time.

Okay, we're at the start of a race. We're in the starting blocks ready to blast out. We hear the gun and we're off. In a few seconds, we're at top speed, racing toward the finish line. But what happened during those first few steps?

The answer is that, we sped up. Every stride carried us a bit further than the one before it. Each stride was faster than the previous one. What would it look like if we could tape it and play it back in slow-motion?

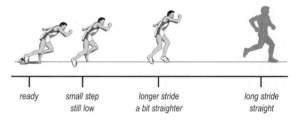

ready   *small step still low*   *longer stride a bit straighter*   *long stride straight*

The tape would show us that for each tick of the clock, we would have traveled a distance. As seen before, d/t is in fact speed. This time, the record would show that the distance traveled per unit of time would <u>not</u> be constant. It would show that each "step" was longer than the one before it.

The first step would be a "baby" step. Hardly noticeable. The next frame would reveal a longer movement followed by an even longer one, etc. For the first few seconds, the distance covered in each click of the slo-mo camera would be longer and longer. Our sensation would be of speeding up. We'd be moving further and further from the starting blocks. But the pattern we saw of time for constant speed goes out the window. The pattern is no longer uniform or steady. So how is our distance-time graph affected by this speeding up?

To make it easier to measure and to see the consistency, let's follow the path of a ball rolling down a ramp. If a picture is taken every tenth of a second, we could then overlap the pictures to show where the ball was each 0.1s from top to bottom. The first all too obvious observation would be that the time went on steadily as the ball rolled downward. It moved farther away from the starting point as time went on. Upon closer examination we would find that the gap, the distance traveled from one flash to the next, is getting larger each 0.1 of a second. Does this make sense?

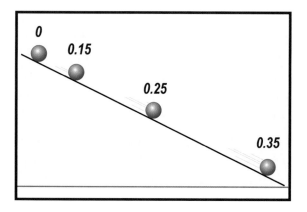

As the ball rolls down the ramp, it does speed up. Speed is how far you travel in

an interval of time. If your speed is faster, the distance must be longer. So far, things seem to be agreeing nicely.

To explore this in greater detail, let's record the data for distance versus time for the ball's movement. The measurements might look something like this.

time (s)	distance (m)
0	0
0.1	0.02
0.3	0.06
0.6	0.14
0.8	0.20
0.9	0.24
1.0	0.30

When we plot this data on our graph, a special picture emerges that describes our speeding up type of movement. It's not the straight line we had last time. If you look at the points, they outline a special pattern, a curve. It begins at (0,0) and then gradually curves upward toward the right. A nice smooth curve! Now, that's different.

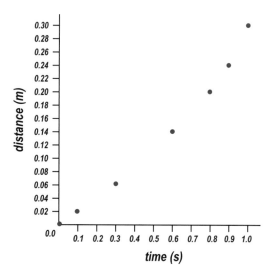

This curve is the graphical picture of our ball speeding up as it moves down the ramp. It probably would describe our movement as we blast out of the starting blocks at the track as well. Somehow, our speeding up is captured in the grace of this curved graph. But how?

Remember last time when our speed stayed constant, so did our graph. It had a constant slope. One steady straight lined slope. What's the story this time? Our speed is constantly changing. What about the graph? Isn't its slope constantly changing as well? It looks like the curve of the graph is telling us that the ball is moving faster and faster. The graph does get steeper and steeper. The ball's "story" is told in the graph's shape.

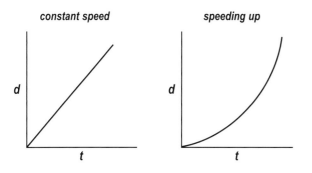

Each tenth of a second seems to have its own slope. In fact, what would happen if we calculated the speed of the ball during each tenth of a second? We'd need to get the distance it traveled <u>during</u> each tenth of a second. That's not as hard to do as it may seem. Watch!

In the first tenth of a second, the ball moved from the starting point 0.02m down the ramp. Ok, that makes the <u>average</u> speed (remember that idea?)

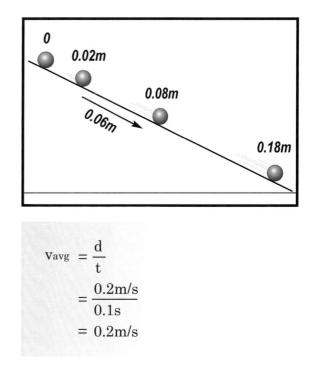

$$V_{avg} = \frac{d}{t}$$
$$= \frac{0.2m/s}{0.1s}$$
$$= 0.2m/s$$

So far so good. Now, it gets a tad trickier.

From the 0.02m position, the ball moves a position 0.08m from the start. In reality, it has moved (0.08 − 0.02)m or 0.06m during the flash of the camera. The distance travelled is 0.06m. The time it took to move this distance is the time between pictures, a tenth of a second. Now, we have both parts for our equation.

Again, $V_{avg} = \frac{d}{t}$
$$= \frac{0.06m}{0.1s}$$
$$= 0.6m/s$$

The ball has a new "average speed". But this V_{avg} is <u>only</u> for the 2nd tenth of a second. Nothing from the 1st tenth is included in it. This gives us the right to say that during the 2nd tenth of a second, the ball is moving at about 0.6 m/s. For that instant in time, that's as fast as it's going.

We can continue this process all the way down the chart and complete a new data table of speed versus time.

Here it is.

time (s)	v_avg (m/s)
0	0
0.1	0.2
0.2	0.6
0.3	1.0
0.4	1.4
0.5	1.8
0.6	2.2
0.7	2.6
0.8	3.0
0.9	3.4
1.0	3.8

According to these values, the ball is moving faster and faster. Just like in the pictures!

Our d-t graph showed the speeding up by curving. The data for the ball's speed shows this increase as well. Now, the question is, how does the v-t graph "tell" the story?

By plotting a graph of velocity versus time, we can see how speeding is pictured graphically.

As we check out the pattern of the points, the curve we saw in the d-t graph is gone. This time, we have our familiar straight line. How does this line tell its story?

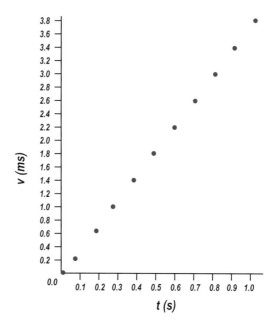

It starts at just about 0. (it's true, it misses by a bit, but for our purposes we don't need to delve that deeply to get the graph to go through (0,0)). From that point onward, it rises. Each tenth of a second, the graph is higher (faster) than before. That certainly describes speeding up but what seems to be happening is that it is rising steadily. The graph has a steady constant slope.

This slope describes the process of speeding up or accelerating. It shows us that the speed keeps on changing. In fact, the speed changes at a very specific rate. This rate is its acceleration. At this point, we need to define some terms to be able to express acceleration correctly.

To begin, we need to find out by how much the speed changes. This value, or concept, even has its own symbol, Δv (read it as delta vee). The Δ symbol simply means "change in." The v part is self explanatory. "Δv" represents the change in speed of an object. The way to get this value is by choosing 2 points to compare. That sounds a lot like doing the slope of the line. Well, it is. By finding Δv, we're taking the first step in calculating the slope of the line.

Back to Δv. To calculate this value, we find the difference between the 2 speeds we've chosen. We always do the 2nd one minus the 1st one, like this.

$$\Delta v = v_2 - v_1$$

With this calculation, we have the object's change in speed. It took time to change the speed, so we calculate the time as well by subtracting the corresponding times.

$$\Delta t = t_2 - t_1$$

Using our previous data, let's choose two pts:

t (s)	v (m/s)
0.3	1.0
0.7	2.6

Our Δv comes out as,
$$\Delta v = v_2 - v_1$$
$$= 2.6\text{m/s} - 1.0\text{m/s}$$
$$= 1.6\text{m/s}$$

And the Δt is,
$$\Delta t = t_2 - t_1$$
$$= 0.7\text{s} - 0.3\text{s}$$
$$= 0.4\text{s}$$

So, here we are. We know the ball's change in speed and we know how long it took to happen. Here's the final piece to the puzzle. Acceleration is defined as "the rate of change in speed." Mathematically we express it as

$$a = \frac{\Delta v}{\Delta t}$$

In our example, it works out as

$$a = \frac{1.6\text{m/s}}{0.4\text{s}}$$
$$= \frac{4 \text{ m/s}}{s}$$

This says, in essense, that the speed is changing at a rate of 4m/s for each second on the ramp. Even though it may be moving for less than a second, we always express acceleration per 1 second.

But you know, that unit looks a bit messy as written. It can be abbreviated as follows.

$$\frac{\text{m/s}}{s} \longrightarrow \text{m/s}^2 \text{ (now, that's better)}$$

This revised unit still expresses the speed factor divided by the time factor but it is compact and convenient.

For the ball accelerating down the ramp, our calculation shows it to be 4m/s^2. But the two points were chosen for you. Choose two of your own points and do the acceleration calculation.

Did you also get 4m/s^2? That's because it was set up so that the ball would accelerate down the ramp at that specific rate. The v-t graph shows that by having a slope of 4m/s^2. Slope is a very powerful thing. On the v-t graph, it shows the acceleration in its straight and constant slope. On the other hand, the d-t graph's slope keeps changing. Since doing the slope on a d-t graph really gives us speed, a changing slope says a change in speed. That's our acceleration.

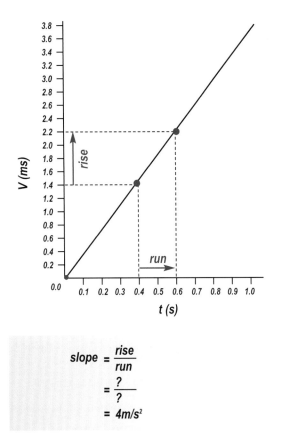

$$slope = \frac{rise}{run}$$

$$= \frac{?}{?}$$

$$= 4m/s^2$$

One final concept is more mathematical. It involves our equation for "a". Try to follow the next few steps.

Start with the definition for acceleration.

$$a = \frac{\Delta v}{\Delta t}$$

but, $\Delta v = v_2 - v_1$

substitute in, $a = \frac{v_2 - v_1}{\Delta t}$

move the Δt, $\quad a\Delta t = v_2 - v_1$

flip the whole equation, $\quad v_2 - v_1 = a\Delta t$

move the v_1 over, $\quad v_2 = v_1 + a\Delta t$

That's it! A new equation. By reading it as a sentence rather than a mathematical formula, it will tell us a lot. It states that the 2nd speed is made of the 1st speed and any additional speed you get from accelerating for some time. Here's a problem to show you how it works.

A car, moving at 10m/s, is accelerated at a rate of $5m/s^2$ over a 4 second period.

What is the car's final speed? Reading the question allows you to set up a list of information. With that organized, a simple substitution leads to the final calculation,

$$v_1 = 10m/s$$
$$a = 5m/s^2$$
$$t = 4s$$
$$v_2 = ?$$

$$v_2 = v_1 + a\Delta t$$
$$= 10m/s + (5m/s^2)\,(4s)$$
$$= 10m/s + 20m/s$$
$$v_2 = 30m/s$$

(you'll note that the units of m x s / s^2 simplify to m/s)

With these tools, the graph, the slope and the equations, you should be able to handle any kind of motion, right? Well, we'll see next section.

Lesson # 5 - Should We Go Faster or Slower?

Objectives:

- Type of motion.

- Effect of slowing down on d-t and v-t graphs.

- How to express deceleration and calculate with it.

To get to this point, we've had to move over a distance during an amount of time. This gave us a way to find out our speed. The equation...

$$v = \frac{d}{t}$$

did that job.

As we saw, that worked great for "whole trips", traveling here, there and everywhere. By combining all the "how fars" and the "how longs," we easily get the "how fast" as it was averaged out. In the second case of cruising along at one speed, the same equation could be used. And once again we could use it for the graph of our constant motion.

We went even farther than that. Even when we changed our speed, we could still use the same equation (although in a limited way) You'd think that Physics can run on only one equation.

Acceleration changed that. We define acceleration as the rate of change in speed. This led to one equation, which comes in 2 forms.

$$a = \frac{\Delta v}{\Delta t}$$
$$\text{and} \quad v_2 = v_1 + a\Delta t$$

We also met a new unit, m/s², but that's not as exciting as the new equations. They begin to open up more possibilities to describe motion.

So, here we are, just about ready to tackle any type of motion, right? Think about it. How many different ways are there? First, we can have <u>no</u> motion. No movement as the clock ticks away. Our d = 0 even though "t" keeps going. Our v = 0

$$\text{because} \quad v = \frac{d}{t} = \frac{0}{t} = 0 = 0$$

And since we have no speed to change, our acceleration is also zero. A tidy package.

Our second way of moving is at a constant rate. Our distance increases steadily as does time. Our "v" doesn't change either once its been set. The flip side of that was not clear when we couldn't pinpoint an exact "v" on our trip down the highway. That could be called variable motion as compared to our uniform motion. We then tackled accelerated motion. To keep it simpler, the acceleration we've used has been constant and steady. How then can we complicate what seems so neat and defined? Let's add one or two wrinkles to the picture.

How do we deal with slowing down? What about going in reverse? Maybe, even in a circle? Not only that, since Physics is supposed to be a science of equations and formulae, where are they? Now, what to start with?

Let's try "slowing down". It's probably a more natural concept to use. You do it all the time. With this idea under our belt, we can analyze the motion as you drive from one stop sign to another for example.

To begin with, isn't there another name we have for slowing down? That's right, <u>deceleration</u>. It's different from acceleration in one basic way: you <u>lose</u> speed rather than gain speed. This will have to change our equations. But wait; let's examine it more closely.

Let's start out at a cruising speed of 10m/s. We're moving at 10m each second, a constant rate. By putting on the brakes, our speed has to go down. Assume, in one second we're down to 8m/s followed by 6m/s the next second. Each second we're traveling more slowly,

moving over a shorter distance each second. If we looked at our distance-time graph, our beautiful straight line would begin to bend, gradually flattening out. The slope would be getting gentler.

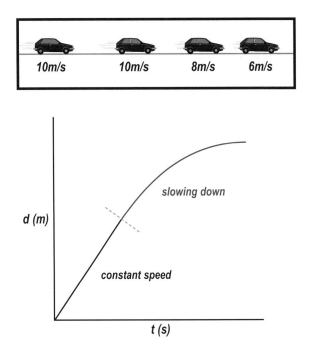

The first impact we can see of our deceleration is a decrease on the speedometer followed by a decrease in the slope of our d-t graph. See the connection?

Next, we examine our v-t graph. At first, we were "cruising" and the graph is nice and steady (flat). Then as we slow down, the graph must show this by decreasing, going "downhill" as it were. If we follow the pattern until we actually stop, the graph will go down in a straight line until it hits 0m/s (meets the time axis).

This line is straight. It has a slope. But it's different than those we met before. Before we take that on, let's talk about deceleration again in preparation.

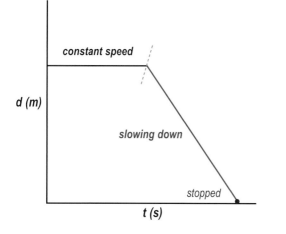

Deceleration means that we're slowing down. Our starting speed, v_1, will be bigger than the next speed we get. By definition, acceleration is the rate of change in speed. Our speed is changing but this time it is decreasing. Our v_2 is less than our v_1. For example, we started at 10m/s and 2 seconds later we're at 6m/s. Do we follow the same rules for calculating acceleration?

Absolutely!

Our change in speed is defined as
$$\Delta v = v_2 - v_1$$

Let's put in our values.
$$\Delta v = 6\text{m/s} - 10\text{m/s}$$
$$= -4\text{m/s}$$

A rather odd value but of major significance. It tells us 2 very important things. One, it states that the speed changed by 4m/s. That part was easy. The second thing it shows us is the "slowing down." How? The value is negative. As in business, a loss is shown as a negative value (also in red as a warning, but in our case there is no danger). The -4m/s tells both of these stories; the amount and that it's a loss.

Our deceleration can now be calculated.

Since $$a = \frac{\Delta v}{\Delta t}$$

Our $\Delta v = -4$m/s and $\Delta t = 2$ seconds
So, $$a = \frac{-4\text{m/s}}{2\text{m/s}}$$
$$a = -2\text{m/s}^2$$

The rate at which we decelerate is -2m/s^2. Translation: we are slowing down, as shown by the negative sign, (the old "take away" sign) and at a rate of 2m/s for each second. We've been calling this a deceleration, which is okay. Physicists on the other hand might say that, in fact, this represents a negative acceleration. Well, both expressions are correct.

Acceleration is defined as the rate of change in speed. Speeding up (accelerating) and slowing down (decelerating) fit this description. The equation

$$a = \frac{\Delta v}{\Delta t}$$

accommodates this without difficulty, now that we know what the – sign refers to. But what about our other equation?

$$v_2 = v_1 + a\Delta t$$

Let's try it out with our present data. How fast are we going after 2 seconds?

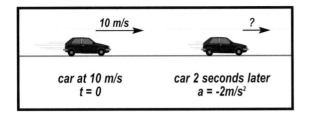

car at 10 m/s
t = 0

car 2 seconds later
a = -2m/s²

We know it's 6m/s but let's see how to calculate it. Our given is

$v_1 = 10m/s$
$a = -2m/s^2$ (our deceleration)
$t = 2s$

and we need to find $v_2 = ?$

$$v_2 = v_1 + a\Delta t$$
substitute in $\quad v_2 = 10m/s + (-2m/s^2)\ (2s)$
simplify $\qquad\ \ v_2 = 10m/s + (-4m/s)$
$\qquad\qquad\quad\ v_2 = 6m/s$ (as stated before)

The equation works for both types of acceleration. The most important point to watch out for is keeping track of the sign. The "−" sign is obvious and is used for deceleration. A "+" sign is generally invisible. For acceleration, speeding up, the "+" sign is understood to be in front of the number.

Let's see if you can handle a bit of stop and go. Here's the problem. You're watching a car go by. It's moving at 12m/s when the driver steps on the accelerator. That gives the car an acceleration of 3m/s² for 2 seconds before the driver has to apply the brakes. That decelerates the car at a rate of 4m/s². He presses the brakes for 1.5s. How fast is the car going at the end of this stop and go? (Remember to use the signs).

Now for the answer. We have to do it in two steps. For the accelerating part we have,

$v_1 = 12m/s$
$a = 3m/s^2$
$t = 2s$
Find $\ v_2 = ?$

$v_2 = v_1 + a\Delta t$
$v_2 = 12m/s + (3m/s^2)\ (2s)$
$v_2 = 12m/s + 6m/s$
$v_2 = 18m/s$

This v_2 will be the starting speed for our deceleration phase, so we'll call it v_1. (You could keep the v_2 and call our final speed v_3 if you'd like instead).

For the braking phase, we have

$v_1 = 18m/s$

$a = -4\ m/s^2$
(add it in even though I left it out)

$t = 1.5s$
find $\ v_2 = ?$
$v_2 = v_1 + a\Delta T$
$v_2 = 18m/s + (-4m/s^2)\ (1.5s)$
$v_2 = 18m/s + (-6m/s)$
$v_2 = 12m/s$

Back to where we started (speed-wise only)

As we've seen, slowing down is the flip side of speeding up. Everything works the same as long as you keep track of the signs (+/-).

In the next section, we will continue this speeding up/slowing down analysis to see how we can figure out how far we've traveled while it was going on. We'll also try to tackle going backwards.

_____
_____
_____
_____
_____
_____
_____
_____
_____
_____
_____
_____
_____
_____
_____
_____
_____
_____
_____
_____
_____
_____
_____
_____
_____
_____
_____
_____
_____
_____
_____
_____
_____

Lesson # 6 - Which Way Did He Go?

Objectives:

- How to use the v-t graph to find distance traveled.

- How area under a curve describes distance traveled.

- A brand new equation for motion.

In the last section, we dealt with both speeding up and slowing down. They both fall under the category of acceleration but we have a more common word for decreasing our speed, deceleration. Both of these affect the v-t graph. When we were cruising along, the graph was flat. As we sped up, the graph had a slope upward. The deceleration was represented by the graph's line heading downward.

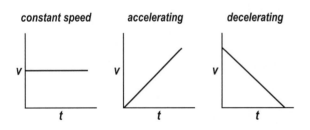

constant speed   accelerating   decelerating

It would seem that the V-t graph tells a very complete story. Let's see how far the story can go. Remember, we also have to be able to see how <u>far</u> we've gone on the graph. And to add a new wrinkle, how could we show ourselves moving backwards? Can the V-t graph show us all that? Well, yes it can and here's how.

Recall how we got started. A simple equation connected how far?, how long?, and how fast?

$$v = \frac{d}{t}$$

Or in its other more useful form,

D = vt

Let's examine this one more closely.

This equation "says" that to get the distance traveled all you need to do is multiply how fast you were going by how long it took. I hope you remember that this could work for many situations, for example, moving at a constant speed or even over a long trip where you use the average speed. In each case, it comes down to a speed multiplied by an amount of time.

Okay, where else have you had to multiply one value times another? Never mind things like figuring out the tax on a new pair of shoes. Think outside the box. Actually, think about a box. When you calculate the area of a box's side, you have to multiply the length by the height. That's two values/measurements being multiplied together, just as in our motion equation. Where's the area connection? Watch.

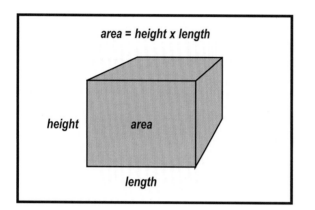

Let's start with our cruising along at 15m/s for say 20 seconds. Sure, it would be easy to get the distance traveled by using the equation,

v = 15m/s
t = 20s
D = ?

d = vt
d = 15m/s 20s
d = 300m

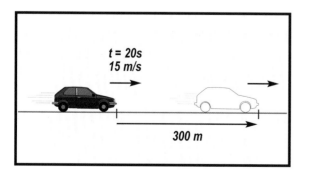

But the graph can give up this information.

The graph is just a flat line across. Nothing special. What if at the end of the line we draw a dotted line straight down to the time axis? It seems we have a rectangle. Its height is the value of the speed. Its length is the amount of time it took. As with other "rectangles," we can find its area.

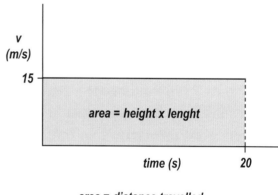

area = distance travelled

area = height x length
     = v x t

But wait, isn't that

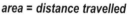

vt = d

Our distance? Yes, it is.

We can say now that the area of the rectangle on the graph matches the distance traveled. Try it.

d = area of rectangle
d = (15m/s) (20s)
d = 300m

Just as before.

You're probably thinking; if we already know the speed and time, why waste time doing the graph and then finding the area? You're right, partially. But what about this example?

A car moving at 8m/s speeds up steadily to 14m/s in a space of 6s. How far did it go during this acceleration?

How do we go about solving this one? Let's try an equation first, then the graph.

Our starting speed, v_1, is 8m/s. By accelerating, we reach a second speed, v_2, of 14m/s.

We could find how fast we were moving at average from 1 to 2 since it was a steady increase. For part of the time we'd be going slower than the average and for part of the time, faster, each part "balancing" out the other. This sounds like the average is in the middle. Well, it is. We get it by doing a simple average of v_1 and v_2.

$$V_{avg} = \frac{v_1 + v_2}{2}$$

This puts v_{avg} right between $v1$ and $v2$.

Using this new equation, we can calculate our distance.

1. $V_{avg} = \dfrac{v_1 + v_2}{2}$

2. $d = v_{avg} \times t$

By putting these together, we get

$$d = \frac{(v_1 + v_2)}{2} \times t$$

Make sure to write the brackets around $(v_1 + v_2)$ and separate the two parts by the multiplication symbol. If you don't and you punch the values straight into your calculator, your answer will be wrong.

On the other hand, there is nothing wrong with doing Vavg first and then placing that value into the equation for distance. Try it that way while we look at the one-step equation.

With the values given, we can plug them into the formula. It should look like this

$$d = \frac{(8m/s + 14m/s)}{2} \times 6s$$

On most calculators, there are buttons like this $\boxed{(}\boxed{)}$. We'll use them in our calculation. To get the distance, punch in the values as follows but clear the screen first.

You should be looking at the same value you got doing it in two steps, 66.

The units do cancel out leaving you with "m."

Final answer, 66m.

How will the graph get us to the same answer? We've got to find out the area of the graph. First, we need to plot the graph. To get our points, we can say that the 8m/s occurred at 0 seconds and that at t=6s, the speed was 14m/s.

T (s)	v (m/s)
0	8
6	14

Since the speed increases steadily between these 2 points, on the graph, we can use a straight line. We plot the points and join them together.

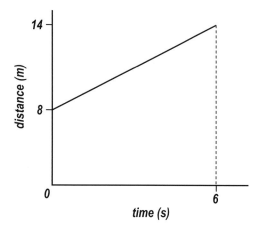

No rectangle, at least not yet. As before, from the end of the graph draw a dotted line down to the time axis. This shape does have an area but it's too complex to work with as is. If you see it already, great. If not, watch what happens when we draw a line across the graph starting at 8m/s (v_1).

What we have done is separate the larger shape into 2 recognizable shapes. A rectangle on the bottom with a triangle atop it. We've already done the area of a rectangle.

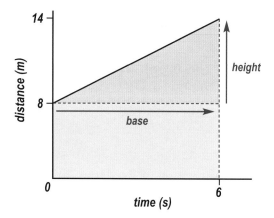

So all that's left is to review how to find the area of a triangle.

Area (triangle) = 1/2 x height x base

For example,

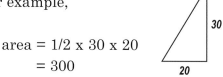

area = 1/2 x 30 x 20
= 300

On our graph, the base is just how long it took from t = 0 to t = 6s. The height on the other hand is a little trickier.

It <u>starts</u> at 8m/s (v_1) and reaches up to 14m/s (v_2). The actual height is:

height = 14m/s − 8m/s
= 6m/s

In variable form, it looks like this:

height = $v_2 - v_1$ which is actually
= Δv

Using the area of a triangle equation, we have

area = 1/2 x height x base
= 1/2 x 6m/s x 6s
= 18m

The distance represented by the triangle is 18m.

In equation form, we just did

area = 1/2 x Δv x t

Back to that later.

Meanwhile, our rectangle is sitting below ready for calculation. Its "height" is 8m/s and its "length" is 6 seconds.

area = height x length
       = 8m/s x 6s
area = 48m

This 48m is the distance the car would have traveled if we hadn't sped up. The total distance traveled is simply the addition of these 2 areas.

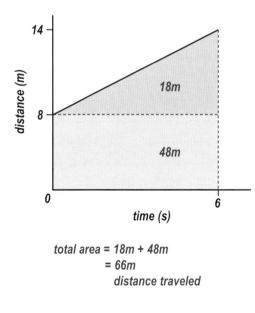

total area = 18m + 48m
           = 66m
           distance traveled

d = area of rectangle + area of triangle
d = 48m + 18m
d = 66m

The same answer that we got before. Confirmation that we did it right. To get more scientific, we can express this using the variables, v_1, etc.

area of rectangle = v_1 x t
area of triangle = 1/2 x Δv x t

The overall equation looks like this

d = v_1t + 1/2 x Δv x t

(As advertised, Physics has lots of equations)

There's just one piece of the equation that needs to be tweaked. That is, Δv. Without too much mathematical manipulation, suffice it to say that the amount of "Δv" is controlled by the acceleration, "a", and the length of time you're accelerating, "t."

These two can replace the Δv in the equation as follows:

d = v_1t + 1/2 x (at) x (t)

Just one more small abbreviation to go. Let's put the 2 "t"s together as t^2 (t squared).

Another rewrite leaves us with the final version of this equation,

d = v_1t + 1/2at^2

That's it! A truly fancy physics equation. Using our original data, let's see how we can get 66m out of it.

Our values were missing the rate of acceleration. Easy enough to calculate though.

$$v_1 = 8\text{m/s}$$
$$v_2 = 14\text{m/s}$$
$$t = 6\text{s}$$
$$a = ?$$

And
$$a = \frac{\Delta v}{t}$$
$$= \frac{(14\text{m/s} - 8\text{m/s})}{6\text{s}}$$
$$a = 1\text{m/s}^2$$

Now let's tackle the equation.

$$d = v_1 t + 1/2at^2$$
$$= (8\text{m/s})\,(6\text{s}) + 1/2 \text{ x } (1\text{m/s}^2)\,(6\text{s})^2$$

The first term gets us a value of 48m. The second term is more delicate though. We have to deal with the squaring of the 6 seconds. You can do that right away and replace the $(6\text{s})^2$ with 36s^2 (units get squared as well).

The second term now looks like this,

$$1/2 \text{ x } (1\text{m/s}^2)\,(36\text{s}^2)$$

Numerically, half of 36 is 18. The units also simplify, as the s^2 cancels out leaving only m. The second term equals 18m. To complete the process, we add them together.

$$d = 48\text{m} + 18\text{m}$$
$$= 66\text{m (again)}$$

How powerful is this V-t graph that lets us use its area and that each area is really just a part of a complex formula.

We are now ready for just about anything. In the last section, we'll use our new equation and graphing skills to deal with the last two twists and turns in motion, how to deal with deceleration and reverse.

Notes

_____
_____
_____
_____
_____
_____
_____
_____
_____
_____
_____
_____
_____
_____
_____
_____
_____
_____
_____
_____
_____
_____

Lesson # 7 - Back It Up

This is it. The final stretch. To complete our final discussion of motion, we will deal with how far we travel while decelerating and/or going backwards. This will show the versatility of v-t graphs and give you your money's worth of using Physics equations.

The two equations we want to carry forward from the last section are

$$d = \frac{(v_1 + v_2)}{2} \times t$$
$$\text{and} \quad d = v_1 t + 1/2 a t^2$$

Along with the v-t graph, we should be able to easily deal with both deceleration and going in reverse.

Let's begin with deceleration. As you recall, deceleration is simply a slowing down process. v_1 decreases until it becomes v_2. When we calculate the Δv, the answer turns out to be negative. Its negative value tells us both the amount of change in speed as well as the fact that it is a decrease. When we

calculate the "a" it also turns out negatively.

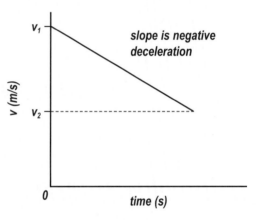

From a value of v_1, it drops to a value of v_2. The slope of this line is negative, as it indicates the negative acceleration (decelerated). But does this interfere with our calculation of the distance travelled? We'll try an example. Our car is moving at 18m/s when we apply the brakes and slow down steadily to 10m/s over a 20 second span. How far did we travel during this braking period?

To get our answer, we'll do it three different ways to show how each can be worked out. The first method will be the simple v_{avg} way. Next, we'll try the area of the graph method, finishing off by using <u>the</u> equation technique.

<u>v_{avg} Method:</u>

v_{avg} Method:

We list our given information to begin with.

$$v_1 = 18\text{m/s}$$
$$v_2 = 10\text{m/s}$$
$$t = 20\text{s}$$
$$d = ?$$

We'll use this equation as a start.

$$d = \frac{(v_1 + v_2)}{2} \times t$$

substituting, $d = \dfrac{(18\text{m/s} + 10\text{m/s})}{2} \times 20\text{s}$

$$d = \frac{(28\text{m/s})}{2} \times 20\text{s}$$
$$d = (14\text{m/s})(20\text{s})$$
$$d = 280\text{m}$$

It looks like this answer totally ignored using a negative sign. Will our other techniques be as easy?

<u>Area of v-t graph:</u>

As we did last time, we create a mini data table with which to plot our graph. The 18m/s at the start will be timed at t = 0s. The 10m/s, which happens later, will be at t = 20s. The table is as follows.

t (s)	v (m/s)
0	18
20	10

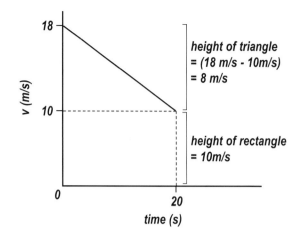

height of triangle
= (18 m/s - 10m/s)
= 8 m/s

height of rectangle
= 10m/s

By plotting these 2 points, we can join them, because we've chosen a smooth, steady braking pattern.

With the graph in place, we put in our dotted lines to create the rectangle and triangle. The rectangle has an area of

area (rectangle) = (10m/s) (20s)
= 200m

Be careful, its height only reaches up to the 10m/s mark.

The triangle has a height of (18m/s – 10m/s) or 8m/s. We'll plug it in to the triangle formula.

area (triangle) = 1/2 x (8m/s) (20s)
= 80m

The total distance traveled is made up of these 2 areas combined.

d = area (rectangle) + area (triangle)
d = 200m + 80m
= 280m

Two methods, each coming up with the same answers. It looks good for our third method, doesn't it?

The Equation:

The equation is as follows:

$$d = v_1t + 1/2at^2$$

Our list of information is missing the value of "a". We'll calculate it before we proceed.

$$a = \frac{\Delta v}{t}$$

and $\Delta v = (v_2 - v_1)$

$$\Delta v = (10m/s - 18m/s)$$
$$\Delta v = -8m/s$$

Since we did slow down, it's to be expected that Δv would be negative. On to the deceleration calculation.

$$a = \frac{\Delta v}{t}$$
$$a = \frac{-8m/s}{20s}$$
$$a = -0.4m/s^2$$

This value is telling us that the speed is changing (decreasing) by 0.4m/s for each second we have the brakes on. It may not be a large number but it's still important.

Now we're ready for the equation.

Again, $d = v_1t + 1/2at^2$

Substituting,
$$d = (18m/s)(20s) + 1/2(-0.4m/s^2)(20s)^2$$

Take care of the first term before we deal with the second one.

$$(18m/s)(20s) = 360m$$
Thus, $d = 360m + 1/2(-0.4m/s^2)(20s)^2$

It appears we may have overshot our 280m distance. Or maybe not?

The 360m came from using the 18m/s for the whole 20 seconds. But that didn't really happen! We were always slowing down, travelling a shorter distance than the second before. We were destined never to reach a 360m total distance.

Examining the second term will explain it. First, do the numerical part. Multiply 1/2 (or 0.5) times (0.4) then by 20^2 (or 400). However you punch it in on the calculator the answer should be 80. The units clean themselves up to be meters. The only thing left is the minus sign.

You recall from basic math, that when you multiply + and − values together, if there is an odd number of negative signs, the answer is negative. That's the case here. Our 80m is really -80m. That's by how much we'll miss traveling 360m.

The second math step, of adding a negative number, has to be done. We do it by simply subtracting.

$$d = 360m + (-80m)$$
becomes $d = 360m - 80m$
$$d = 280m$$

Our final method also gets to the right answer of 280m. By handling the negative sign properly, all techniques agree.

The best (or worst) has been left for last. How are we going to keep track of our comings and goings?

Since we're only introducing the idea in this section, we'll limit our discussion to going forward and then reversing along a fixed track, like a toy train that only moves along straight tracks. In this way, we'll get the idea of how to deal with back and forth.

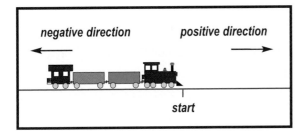

To keep things in perspective, we'll designate going forward as moving in a positive direction. We need this because reverse <u>must</u> be shown as the opposite of forward. If forward is positive then reverse becomes negative.

If the train moves forward (to the right) 1.5m in 2 seconds, we can say it moved at a speed of

$$v = \frac{d}{t}$$
$$= \frac{1.5m}{2s}$$
$$v = 0.75m/s \longrightarrow (+0.75 \text{ m/s})$$

The plus sign was always there before but "invisible." We didn't need it to distinguish direction until now. In many situations, it is important to figure out how far we've <u>actually moved</u> from our starting position. So far, the train is +1.5m, having gotten there at an average speed of +0.75m/s.

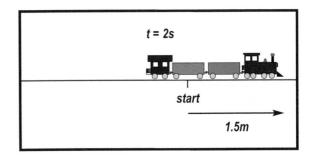

Let's say we stop the train for a second while we get ready to switch it into reverse. We then bring the train back to its starting point more slowly, say, over a 3 second period. The distance travelled is 1.5m but in <u>reverse</u>. Due to the direction, we'll write -1.5m. The time was 3 seconds (note time has no direction).

The speed this time is

$$v = \frac{d}{t}$$
$$= \frac{-1.5m}{3s}$$
$$v = -0.5m/s$$

The value of -0.5m/s tells us two things about the motion. First, the speed is 0.5m/s and in addition, the direction is reversed.

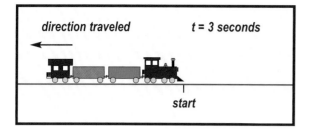

The forward motion has been cancelled by a motion in reverse.

d   forward = +1.5m
d   reverse = -1.5m

How far did the train travel?

We actually have two answers and both can be correct. But first, we <u>must</u> specify what the question "how far?" really refers to. Do we mean, how far, in total, did the train go? This is similar to our "whole trip" type of problem. The second way to phrase the question is, how far did the train get to (from its starting point to its final position)?

One answer comes out to be 3m while the other is zero. Ever run into this kind of duality before? You probably have.

Say you were to borrow the family car without asking. You drive to your friend's house and then to the mall then back home. You're asked "where did you go?" Your answer will probably be "nowhere," right? You add, "See, the car's right where you left it."

You do realize there's a flaw in this plan. All your parents have to do is check the odometer. If they jotted down what it started at, a simple calculation will give them the "how far?" of your trip. Your answer of "nowhere" is true for how far you got from <u>start</u> to <u>finish</u> but won't get you out of paying for the gas, etc.

By adding this idea of direction to our powerful v-t graph, watch how awesome it truly becomes.

Using the train data, and assuming a constant speed up and down the track, the graph should look as follows.

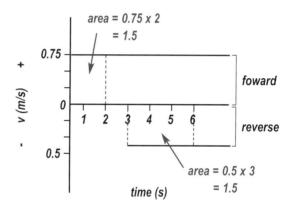

For the first time, we have to extend the speed axis <u>below</u> the time axis. This allows us to show the forward <u>and</u> the reverse motion on the same graph.

The graph has two rectangles, one on the + side and one on the − side. As before, each area represents how far the train traveled in each direction. Now, we can answer either question ⟶ how far? or how far did it get?

We can go on to see how accelerating and decelerating backwards and forwards also works, but I think this section and this whole chapter is a large enough introduction to motion to keep you going.

Re-read this chapter from the beginning to end to see how all these parts fit together. This way you'll have a good foundation for checking out just about any kind of movement you observe or participate in.

Unit 3 – Questions

1. What two things must happen together for it to be called motion?

_____

_____

_____

2. What objects move that are hard to notice?

_____

_____

_____

3. What are the two questions that we ask to establish movement?

_____

_____

_____

4. If a rabbit hopped 5 meters in 2 seconds, how fast was it going?

_____

_____

5. If you drive 80 km in 1-hour, stop for 15 min., then drive back in 45 min., what is your average speed for this trip?

_____

_____

6. What is the slope of this graph?

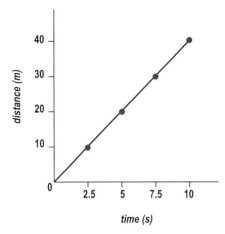

7. How do you know an object is stopped by using the distance-time graph?

_____

8. When speeding up, what are the shapes of the d-t and v-t graph?

_____

9. A skateboarder rolled down a ramp. He accelerated at 2m/s². He pushed off at 8m/s and it took 0.75 seconds to reach the bottom. How fast was he going at the bottom?

_____

10. A bus moving at 16m/s must slow down for traffic. The traffic is moving at 12m/s. The driver has 0.5 seconds to apply the brakes. What is the rate of deceleration?

_____

11. From the following graph, determine the distance traveled.

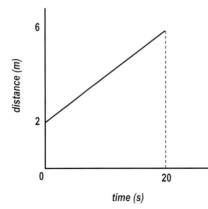

12. If a car is decelerated at $3m/s^2$ from a speed of 18m/s, how far will it travel during 4 seconds of braking?

Notes

Answers to Questions

UNIT 1: ELECTRICITY

1. Dalton

2. attract because they have opposite charges
   repel because they have the same charge

3. pith ball and gold-leaf

4. separate charges by moving electrons to the cathode (- pole) away from the anode (+ pole)

5. solar energy; electromagnetic induction; piezoelectricity

6. power source, connecting wires & circuit element (switch is optional)

7. ammeter – measures current
   voltmeter – measures potential difference

8. a) voltage – voltages add up to the total
   b) resistance – resistances add up to the total

9.

	V =	I x	R
#1	20V	2 A	10 Ω
#2	40V	2 A	20 Ω
Total	60V	2 A	30 Ω

10. a) voltage – all voltages are the same
    b) current – currents add up to the total

11.

	V =	I x	R
#1	30V	2 A	15 Ω
#2	30V	1 A	30 Ω
Total	30V	3 A	10 Ω

12. parallel

13. circuit breakers/fuses

UNIT 2: SIMPLE MACHINES: FORCE AND WORK

1. x-y axis, geographic N/S/E/W and circle (0°-360°)

2. $\dfrac{250g}{1000} = 0.25kg$ $F_g = mg$

    $\qquad\qquad\qquad = (0.25kg)\,(10m/s^2)$
    $\qquad\qquad\qquad = 2.5N$

3. $F_a = 25N$ work $= F_d$
    $\;\;d = 3m$ $\qquad = (25N)\,(3m)$
    $\qquad\qquad\;\; = 75J$

4. $F_g = mg$ work $= (30N)\,(1.2m)$
    $\quad = 3.10$ $\qquad = 36J$
    $\quad = 30N$
    $..d = 1.2m$

5. IMA = 3   AMA = 3 $AMA = \dfrac{F_r}{F_e}$

    $F_e = 5N$ $3 = \dfrac{F_r}{5}$

    $\qquad\qquad\qquad F_r = 15N$

6. $\text{Work}_{output} = (F_r)\,(d_r)$
    $\qquad\qquad = (20N)\,(1.5m)$
    $\qquad\qquad = 30J \quad \text{which equals work}_{input}$
    $\qquad 30J = (F_e)\,(d_e)$
    $\qquad 30J = (F_e)\,(6m)$
    $\qquad\; F_e = 5N$

7. 4

8. $IMA = AMA$
    $\qquad 5 = \dfrac{200}{F_e}$
    $\qquad F_e = 40N$

9. • wedge, axe, screw for example
    • nutcracker, fishing rod, etc.
    • block and tackle, car hoist

UNIT 3: SIMPLE MOTION

1. a change in position and a length of time.

2. the moon, the continents, an atom, etc.

3. how far? and how long?

4. 2.5 m/s

5. 80 km/hr

6. 4 m/s

7. graph is flat

8.

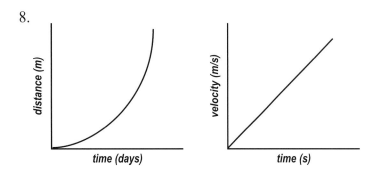

9. 9.5 m/s

10. -8m/s^2

11. 80m

12. 48m

Glossary

Acceleration – The time rate of change of velocity with respect to magnitude or direction; the derivative of velocity with respect to time.

Atom – The smallest component of an element having the chemical properties of the element, consisting of a nucleus containing combinations of neutrons and protons and one or more electrons bound to the nucleus by electrical attraction; the number of protons determines the identity of the element.

Battery – Also called galvanic battery, voltaic battery. A combination of two or more cells electrically connected to work together to produce electric energy.

Block and tackle – The ropes or chains and blocks used in a hoisting tackle.

Cathode ray – A flow of electrons emanating from a cathode in a vacuum tube and focused into a narrow beam.

Circuit – Also called electric circuit. The complete path of an electric current, including the generating apparatus, intervening resistors, or capacitors.

Current – The time rate of flow of electric charge, in the direction that a positive moving charge would take and having magnitude equal to the quantity of charge per unit time: measured in amperes.

Deceleration – A decrease in velocity.

Displacement – The linear or angular distance in a given direction between a body or point and a reference position.

Distance – The interval between two points.

Electric charge – One of the basic properties of the elementary particles of matter giving rise to all electric and magnetic forces and interactions. The two kinds of charge are given negative and positive algebraic signs: measured in coulombs.

Electrical potential – Also called potential. The work done per unit charge in moving an infinitesimal point charge from a common reference point to the given point.

Electron – An elementary particle that is a fundamental constituent of matter, having a negative charge of 1.602×10^{-19} coulombs, a mass of 9.108×10^{-31} kilograms, and existing independently or as the component outside the nucleus of an atom.

Electroscope – A device for detecting the presence and determining the sign of electric charges by means of electrostatic attraction and repulsion, often between two pieces of gold leaf enclosed in a glass-walled chamber.

Glossary

Electrostatics – The branch of physics dealing with electric phenomena not associated with electricity in motion.

Element – One of a class of substances that cannot be separated into simpler substances by chemical means.

Equation – An expression or a proposition, often algebraic, asserting the equality of two quantities.

Force – An influence on a body or system, producing or tending to produce a change in movement or in shape or other effects.

Friction – Surface resistance to relative motion, as of a body sliding or rolling.

Graph – A diagram representing a system of connections or interrelations among two or more things.

Inclined Plane – One of the simple machines, a plane surface inclined to the horizon, or forming with a horizontal plane any angle but a right angle.

Induction – The process by which a body having electric or magnetic properties produces magnetism, an electric charge, or an electromotive force in a neighboring body without contact.

Joule – The SI unit of work or energy, equal to the work done by a force of one newton when its point of application moves through a distance of one meter in the direction of the force: equivalent to 107 ergs and one watt-second.

Kilogram – A unit of mass equal to 1000 grams: the base SI unit of mass, equal to the mass of the international prototype of the kilogram, a platinum-iridium cylinder kept in Sèvres, France.

Lever – A rigid bar that pivots about one point and that is used to move an object at a second point by a force applied at a third.

Machine – An apparatus consisting of interrelated parts with separate functions, used in the performance of some kind of work: A device that transmits or modifies force or motion. Also called simple machine. Any of six or more elementary mechanisms, as the lever, wheel and axle, pulley, screw, wedge, and inclined plane.

Magnitude – Size; extent; dimensions.

Mechanical Advantage – Any state, circumstance, opportunity, or means specially favorable to success, interest, or any desired end: having to do with machinery.

Model – A simplified representation of a system or phenomenon, as in the sciences or economics, with any hypotheses required to describe the system or explain the phenomenon, often mathematically.

Motion – The action or process of moving, or of changing place or position; movement.

Movement – The act, process, or result of moving.

Newton – The SI unit of force, equal to the force that produces an acceleration of one meter per second on a mass of one kilogram.

Ohm – The SI unit of electrical resistance, defined to be the electrical resistance between two points of a conductor when a constant potential difference applied between these points produces in this conductor a current of one ampere. The resistance in ohms is numerically equal to the magnitude of the potential difference. Symbol, Ω.

Origin – The point in a Cartesian coordinate system where the axes intersect.

Position – Condition with reference to place; location; Power a. – Work done or energy transferred per unit of time. Symbol, P. b. The time rate of doing work.

Pulley – A wheel, with a grooved rim for carrying a line, that turns in a frame or block and serves to change the direction of or to transmit force, as when one end of the line is pulled to raise a weight at the other end: one of the simple machines.

Resistance – Also called ohmic resistance. A property of a conductor by virtue of which the passage of current is opposed, causing electric energy to be transformed into heat: equal to the voltage across the conductor divided by the current flowing in the conductor: usually measured in ohms.

Slope – The derivative of the function whose graph is a given curve evaluated at a designated point.

Speed – Relative rapidity in moving, going, etc.; rate of motion or progress:

Uniform motion – Constant, unvarying, undeviating, motion

Valence electron – An electron of an atom, located in the outermost shell of the atom, that can be transferred to or shared with another atom.

Variable – A quantity or function that may assume any given value or set of values.

Voltage – Electromotive force or potential difference expressed in volts.

Watt – The SI unit of power, equivalent to one joule per second and equal to the power in a circuit in which a current of one ampere flows across a potential difference of one volt.

Wedge – A piece of hard material with two principal faces meeting in a sharply acute angle, for raising, holding, or splitting objects by applying a pounding or driving force, as from a hammer.

Glossary

Weight – The force that gravitation exerts upon a body, equal to the mass of the body times the local acceleration of gravity: commonly taken, in a region of constant gravitational acceleration, as a measure of mass.

Wheel and axle – A simple machine consisting, in its typical form, of a cylindrical drum to which a wheel concentric with the drum is firmly fastened: ropes are so applied that as one unwinds from the wheel, another rope is wound on to the drum.

Work – Force times the distance through which it acts; specifically, the transference of energy equal to the product of the component of a force that acts in the direction of the motion of the point of application of the force and the distance through which the point of application moves.